Creative Smocking

Creative Smocking

Contemporary Design
Traditional Techniques

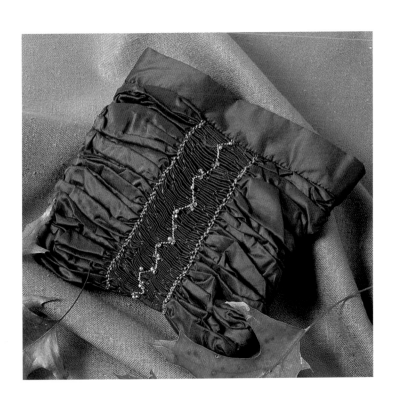

Chris Rankin

LARK BOOKS

A Division of
Sterling Publishing Co., Inc.
New York

Creative Smocking

EDITOR: **Carol Parks**

DESIGN AND PRODUCTION: **Chris Bryant**

PHOTOGRAPHY: **Evan Bracken**
Morley F. Johnson, *pages 99, 101, 103, 108*

ILLUSTRATIONS: **Bernadette Wolf**

EDITORIAL ASSISTANCE: **Valerie Anderson, Laura Doran**

Library of Congress Cataloging-in-Publication Data

Rankin, Chris.
    Creative smocking: contemporary designs, traditional techniques / Chris Rankin.
        p.   cm.
    Includes index.
    ISBN 1-887374-33-7 (hbk) ISBN 1-57990-386-x (pbk)
    1. Smocking. I. Title
TT840.S66R36   1997
746.44—dc21

97-4054
CIP

10 9 8 7 6 5 4 3 2 1

Published by Lark Books, a division of
Sterling Publishing Co., Inc.
387 Park Avenue South, New York, N.Y. 10016

First Paperback Edition 2002
© 1997 Lark Books

Distributed in Canada by Sterling Publishing,
c/o Canadian Manda Group, One Atlantic Ave., Suite 105
Toronto, Ontario, Canada M6K 3E7

Distributed in the U.K. by:
Guild of Master Craftsman Publications Ltd.
Castle Place, 166 High Street, Lewes East Sussex, England BN7 1XU
Tel: (+ 44) 1273 477374, Fax: (+ 44) 1273 478606,
Email: pubs@thegmcgroup.com, Web: www.gmcpublications.com

Distributed in Australia by Capricorn Link (Australia) Pty Ltd., P.O. Box 704, Windsor, NSW 2756 Australia

If you have questions or comments about this book, please contact:
Lark Books
67 Broadway
Asheville, NC 28801
(828) 236-9730

Printed in China

ISBN 1-887374-33-7 (hbk) ISBN 1-57990-386-x (pbk)

CONTENTS

INTRODUCTION

▲ Strictly decorative smocking, worked on a separate fabric piece then appliquéd to the blouse front, adds design interest without altering the sleek lines of the garment. This lattice pattern is worked in the Canadian, or North American, smocking technique described on page 50.

Smocking is one of the oldest forms of fabric manipulation—the shaping of fabric with pleats and stitches. Hundreds of years ago, when the construction of a garment often began with rectangular pieces of fabric in various sizes, smocking was used to gather up the fabric fullness at those points where fitting was necessary. The fabric was simply pleated up and stitched decoratively to hold it to shape. Some of the earliest examples of smocked clothing were undergarments and shirts, heavily embellished and worn by the upper classes. The more familiar smock became popular in later centuries as a farm worker's or laborer's garment, sometimes waterproofed and worn to protect the clothing.

With the trend in this century toward sleeker styles, smocking has come to be associated mainly with delicate dresses for little girls. The advent of elastic has eliminated the need for smocking as a functional technique to control fabric fullness. Fashion and cost-consciousness of the garment industry have all but eliminated decorative stitchery on ready-to-wear. And most women who do sew for themselves and their families rarely can spare extra time to add elaborate hand-stitched embellishment to everyday garments.

Yet in the past few years embellishment of handmade clothing and household items is becoming increasingly popular. Perhaps the trend is due to a desire for individual expression at a time when the fashion in clothing and accessories is for very simple lines and minimal adornment. Perhaps, too, the increased capabilities of sewing machines makes faster work of the functional aspects of sewing and leave a little more time for creative fun.

▲ There are all sorts of ways to incorporate smocking into a project. On this simple neckroll pillow, the end sections are separate pieces, cut approximately four times the width of the central section to allow for the smocking pleats. Corded piping highlights the seamlines and shadow work decorates the central panel.

Smocking has become very popular not just in its traditional form, but as an experimental technique for fiber artists and adventurous sewers who enjoy creating one-of-a-kind garments. It is increasingly used for an accent rather than as an overall design. It is mixed with other stitching techniques and with other forms of embroidery. Beading is added. Ribbon is incorporated into the design or used for the smocking itself. The neat, symmetrical pleats of traditional smocking are distorted and reconfigured in all directions.

The vast array of decorative threads that have become available during the past few years have enticed many stitchers to try smocking for the first time. Fascinating effects can be achieved when traditional stitches are worked with metallics, or interwoven with silk ribbon. Silk thread is no longer difficult to find and creates an absolutely elegant effect when used to smock silk fabric.

In spite of its intricate appearance, smocking isn't the least bit difficult to do. The traditional stitches are few. They are easy to learn and quick to work, and the potential for creative combinations is nearly limitless.

On the following pages you will see dozens of examples of smocking, illustrating a variety of ways that the techniques can be used. It is hoped that our designs will inspire your own and that they will provide you with not just with the basic skills, but with countless ideas for using smocking in innovative ways.

Preparing to Stitch

Part of the joy of smocking is that something beautiful can
be created with few supplies and with no special tools.
Almost any decorative thread, almost any light- or
medium-weight fabric, and away you go. With several
smocking techniques it is not even necessary to
pre-pleat the fabric before you start to stitch.

Thread for Smocking

VIRTUALLY ANY EMBROIDERY thread can be used to work the traditional smocking stitches. Cotton floss and pearl cotton are good choices and are easy to manage. Lustrous silk thread and glittery metallics create interesting special effects. Mixing threads—a strand of cotton floss with a fine metallic, for example, can also produce some pretty stitching. Narrow silk ribbon and fine embroidery wool can give a whole new dimension to simple traditional stitches.

Choose thread that is compatible with the fabric and the overall design. Finer threads look best with delicate designs and intricate patterns. Heavy threads create bold stitching patterns, attractive with coarsely woven fabrics and those with heavier texture.

Six-strand cotton embroidery floss is a universal favorite. It is readily available in every conceivable color, it's inexpensive, and it is easy to use. For most fabrics and stitch patterns, three strands are used for smocking. Two strands might be better for a delicate design worked on cotton or silk batiste. Four strands are often used to produce the solid coverage desirable for picture smocking or for a bold design.

Remember that embroidery floss, like sewing thread, has a nap, or grain. Pull the strand lightly between your thumb and finger and you will feel that it is smoother when pulled in one direction than in the other. Thread the needle with the smooth end—so that you will be pulling the thread through the cloth in the direction that it is smoothest. This simple measure will go a long way toward preventing the aggravation of knotted thread. Cut the end of the thread at an angle to slip it more easily through the needle's eye.

▲ Silk threads and metallics impart a light-refracting quality to the stitches. Glass seed beads and surface embroidery with silk ribbon are wonderfully compatible embellishments.

► Stranded cotton embroidery floss and pearl cotton are versatile favorites for smocking.

For pleating up the fabric, use strong sewing thread. If the piece of fabric is fairly small, or if the fabric is delicate, use standard weight polyester thread. With heavier fabrics and very wide pieces, quilting thread or heavier polyester thread might be safer. It is a time-consuming process, especially if a pleater is used, to start over when a gathering thread breaks.

Needles

FOR MOST FABRICS and the standard three strands of floss a number 8 crewel needle is a good choice. With coarser fabrics and pearl cotton or four or more strands of floss, try a number 5 needle. A number 9 will work with one or two strands of floss and for very fine fabric.

Hand sewing needles, like machine needles, eventually become dull. If the needle has been dropped periodically on the floor or has been used to sew on buttons, get rid of it and find a new one. Fine silk and batiste especially are vulnerable to damage with a blunt needle.

Choosing a Fabric

THE SMOCKED PIECES shown throughout this book were worked on wool flannel, silk charmeuse, denim, polyester satin, corduroy, stiff silk taffeta, fine handkerchief linen, and crisp cotton organdy in addition to those fabrics more often associated with the technique. Almost any light- to medium-weight material is a candidate for smocking. What's important is to know how the fabric will pleat, how it will behave when you stitch upon it, and how it will look when it is finished.

Even-weave fabrics are easiest to manage. Best for most projects are fabrics that drape nicely and aren't too stiff. The fabric should hold the pleats in a nicely rounded fashion. The finished smocked piece can't be ironed, so try to choose a fabric that won't crease in an unattractive fashion.

For beginners, fairly lightweight cotton or cotton/polyester fabrics are a good choice. Cotton lawn is delightful to work with. Gingham, in either all cotton or cotton/polyester, is a traditional fabric for smocking, as is dotted Swiss.

Lightweight linen is delightful to work with and makes a beautiful finished piece. If the fabric is too light in weight, though, the pleats can crease rather than keep a smoothly rounded shape.

Don't be afraid to try silk. The luster, "hand'" and drape of many silk fabrics makes them particularly suitable for smocking. Dupion silk, with its beautifully irregular surface and soft sheen, is the choice of many designers whose work appears on these pages. Silk fabrics are not necessarily expensive. Dupionni and noil cost no more than fairly good cotton.

▲ Silk broadcloth, silk crepe, dupion silk, cotton lawn, silk/cotton blends, and soft wool challis are the kinds of fabrics that perform well with smocking.

Many natural or pale-colored silks are washable; the bright colored fabrics are best dry cleaned. All silks will shrink, however, and the fabric must be preshrunk if it is to be used for a project that will be washed.

Wool, although it is not frequently used for smocking projects, can produce some beautiful results. Choose a lightweight plain weave fabric, such as lightweight flannel or challis. Check that it drapes well, and that it is soft rather than crisp. Wool and cotton or wool and rayon challis, too, are marvelous for smocking.

Certain fabrics are best used by experienced smockers. Velvet and other napped fabrics, denim, corduroy, and slippery silks require a little more patience in the pleating and some agility in the stitching.

Avoid at all costs using fabrics that have a checked or plaid pattern that is printed rather than woven. A look at the wrong side will tell you which is the case. Prints are never aligned with the fabric grain, and the resulting smocked piece will have a skewed appearance.

Do use good quality fabric. With smocking, as for any needlework project, a lot of your valuable time will be invested in the work. With inferior fabric the piece you create will never be the treasure it might have been. Besides, working with a wonderful piece of fabric is a pleasure in itself.

How Much Fabric?

AS A GENERAL RULE, start with fabric approximately three times the planned width of the finished smocked section. Very lightweight materials, such as silk or cotton batiste, with a dense stitching pattern may require fabric four to six times the width of the smocked area. Some stitch patterns, such as counterchange, take only about twice the width.

If you aren't sure how your chosen fabric will work, pleat up a sample of the fabric, or one of similar weight. Stitch it with the design you plan to use for the project itself.

Preparing the Fabric

IF THE PLANNED project will be laundered, the fabric should be preshrunk before you begin. This simply means to wash and dry it as you will wash and dry the finished item. Press the laundered fabric with the lengthwise grain, taking care not to distort it.

Laundering beforehand also removes sizing and finishing agents that are often used on cottons especially. Some fabrics are finished heavily enough to make stitching on them difficult.

Straighten the cut edges. With a check or plaid, just trim along the pattern. For solids and prints, pull a crossgrain thread near each end. Clip into the selvage at the desired point, draw out a single thread, and cut along the line that results.

Make sure the fabric grain is straight, with the crossgrain threads exactly perpendicular to the selvages. To do this, fold the fabric in half lengthwise after the cut ends have been trimmed. The selvages should line up, the ends should line up, and there should be no diagonal wrinkles apparent. If this is not the case, try adjusting the piece by pulling diagonally at the "short" corners, and/or steam pressing it. Synthetic blend fabrics may not respond to this treatment; such pieces are better left for another project.

Overcast the raw edges of the piece if it is likely to fray with all the handling. If you are using a pleater, pleat the fabric first and stitch around the fabric edges before drawing up the pleats.

Very soft fabrics, very lightweight fabrics, and slippery fabrics can be tricky to manoeuver through the pleater. A light application of spray starch will give these materials a little body.

Pleating the Fabric

MOST SMOCKING PATTERNS require that the fabric be pleated up beforehand. When smocks were worn by farm laborers to keep their clothing clean, pleats were made by working evenly spaced gathering rows, counting threads between the stitches taken to form the pleats. Fabric can still be pleated this way, but fortunately there easier methods.

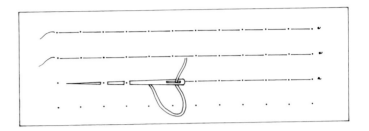

A smocking pleater is the most efficient means of accomplishing the task, but it is not an inexpensive machine. Shops that sell smocking supplies usually will pleat the fabric for you for a small fee. Some mail order suppliers also offer this service.

For a small first project, perhaps a sampler, it can be a worthwhile experience to mark the dots and pleat the fabric manually. Then if you enjoy smocking enough to buy a pleater in the future you will appreciate it all the more.

TRANSFER DOTS

Iron-on transfer dots are available from specialty shops and mail order suppliers of smocking materials. The dots are arranged in rows approximately ⅜ inch (1 cm) apart and spaced at intervals of ¼ inch (.7 cm).

Iron-on dots are generally indelible, so are not a good choice for sheer fabrics because they could show through to the front of the work. As with any iron-on, they should be tested on a scrap of the chosen fabric.

Allow for an extra row of dots (and gathering) above and below the design area of the smocking. Press the dots onto the wrong side of the fabric according to the manufacturer's instructions, with the horizontal rows precisely on the fabric cross grain.

For gathering up the pleats, use strong sewing thread. Beginning always at the same end, "pick up" each dot by taking a small stitch through it. Cut the thread at the end of the row, but don't knot it. Gather the fabric and tie off the pleats as described on page 16.

SMOCKING TEMPLATES

Plastic templates are available with several rows of holes at the appropriate intervals. Dots can be marked onto the fabric and picked up according to the guidelines for using transfer dots.

Use a washable fabric marking pen or washable quilter's pencil to mark the dots. A marker with disappearing ink should not be used as the dots may disappear sooner than you wish, and may rub off as you work on the piece.

Test the removal of the ink on your particular fabric. Cool water removes the marks, but with certain fabric dyes or finishing agents the marks will return, sometimes when the fabric is pressed. If this is the case, repeat the rinsing several times, or wash the fabric with soap or detergent.

PLEATING SHORTCUTS

If you have never tried smocking and don't wish to invest in any special materials, start with a fabric that will help with the pleating. Choose gingham with woven checks approximately ¼ inch (.7 cm) in size. Adopt one corner of each check as a dot, then pick up dots and gather the fabric as if you had used transfer dots.

Fabric with even stripes that size will work, too. The stripes must be woven, not printed, and it will be necessary to mark the horizontal lines. Space them evenly, about ⅜ inch (1 cm) apart, and exactly perpendicular to the stripes.

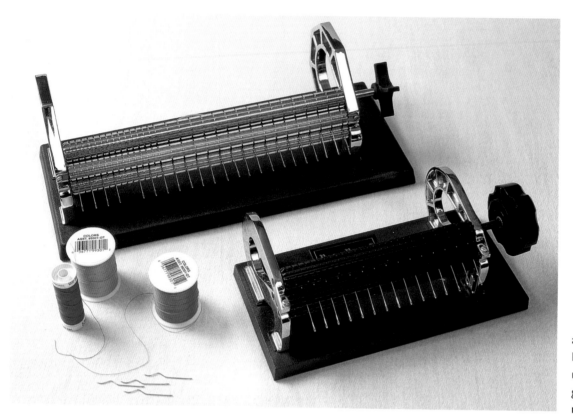

◀ A 24-row and a 16-row pleater. Needles can be removed where gathering lines are not needed.

The Pleater

THE SMOCKING PLEATER eliminates the task of marking dots and gathering up the pleats by hand. It consists of two sets of long gears. One set forms pleats as the fabric is rolled through it. The other set, equipped with needles, stitches through the fabric at the correct intervals at the same time.

The pleater size—and price—is determined by the number of rows it can pleat simultaneously. Models with pleating capacities of 16, 24, and 32 rows are the most widely used. Needles are spaced ⅜ inch (1 cm) apart. Needles can be inserted at some half-space increments as well for additional gathering lines. This is a useful feature with intricate stitch patterns, small items, and very lightweight fabrics.

Most pleaters are operated by means of a hand crank. The state-of-the art model is powered by an electric motor, a time-saver for very serious smockers. Thread racks also are available for some pleaters, making it unnecessary to cut lengths of thread for each pleating job.

The spacing of the stitches made by each needle determines the depth of each pleat, which in turn is determined by the depth of the grooves in the gears that form the pleats. Stitch length, and pleat depth, very from model to model, ranging from 3.6 to 4.3 pleats per inch of fabric.

USING A PLEATER

A successful machine-pleating job depends to a great extent on careful preparation of the fabric beforehand. For most smocking designs, the pleats should be precisely on the lengthwise fabric grain and the gathering lines on the crosswise grain. To accomplish this,the fabric grain must be straight (see page 12).

Most pleaters are sensitive about thick places in the fabric, such as seams and selvages. The fabric won't feed evenly at these points and uneven pleating will result. Trim away the fabric selvages if they are dense enough that a pin won't penetrate them easily.

So that seams won't be too bulky for the pleater to manage, choose lightweight fabric for a design requiring that seams be sewn before the fabric is pleated. Make a very narrow French seam, or trim seam allowances closely. Work carefully past the seam as the fabric is pleated.

Mark off the area that will be pleated. Plan for an upper line of gathering above the top of the design area just inside the seamline. Allow a gathering row below the design area as well. On the pleater, insert only as many needles as you need lines of gathering.

Thread the needles. For each needle, cut a length of thread approximately half as long as the fabric width. If you will pleat more rows than the pleater can do at once, cut the threads slightly longer than the fabric width.

If smocking will be done just on a central area of the fabric piece, at the center of a blouse front section for example, then mark the sides of the design area too. After the piece has been pleated, pull out the threads to the marked lines at each side of the area and tie them off there.

Most manufacturers suggest wrapping the fabric around a length of dowel for pleating. The dowel, with fabric, must slip through the openings in the end plates. Tape one selvage edge of the fabric to the dowel, keeping the fabric edge absolutely straight.

If your design calls for more smocked rows than your pleater can manage, just pleat the fabric in sections. For the first run, cut thread for the needles 6 inches (15 cm) or so longer than the fabric width. Tape the fabric to the dowel as above, and carefully mark the location of the fabric edge.

Pleat the first section. Press the fabric absolutely flat, using a damp pressing cloth if necessary. Measure for the position of the first row of gathering for the second section.

Mark a guideline across the fabric. Position the fabric at the marked line on the dowel to pleat it.

When this section has been pleated, draw up the pleats of the previous section by hand to tie them off. Block the piece as described below.

GET TO KNOW YOUR PLEATER

The first time you use the pleater, try pleating a piece of lightweight checked fabric. You will be able to see whether the fabric feeds evenly through the machine, keeping the stitched rows straight with the crossgrain of the fabric. You can also experiment with controlling the pleater, making deeper or shallower pleats.

If the pleating is uneven, try holding the fabric back slightly at the point where the pleater is using the fabric at a greater rate. If less fabric is taken in to the machine at some point, ease in a little more fabric at that place. Note the extent to which you can control the pleat depth by easing back on the fabric as it feeds, or encouraging the needles to take bigger bites.

PLEATER PLAY

The pleater has hidden talents as a fabric manipulation device and can create some unusual effects. Experiment with the capabilities of your model. Try distorting the pleats this way and that. Striped and checked fabrics, especially, can be altered in the most interesting ways.

Steaming, described below, will set the pleats almost permanently in certain materials. Soft wool flannel, cotton organdy, some polyesters, and stiffer silk fabrics can be manoeuvered in this way for special effects.

PLEATER NEEDLES

Like sewing machine needles, pleater needles become dull with use. A dull needle can damage sheer fabric in addition to causing difficulties in the use of the machine. Needles are not meant to last forever; they will need to be replaced occasionally. Keep the reasonably good ones in a separate place for use with less sensitive fabrics and use new ones for silks and sheers. If a needle is bent or the point breaks, throw it away.

FINISHING THE PLEATS

After the fabric has been pleated, draw up the threads so the pleated fabric is the width you require. Pin the piece to the ironing board, placing a pin at the knotted end of each gathering thread and keeping the pins in a perfectly straight vertical line. Measure the across the piece at each gathering row and adjust the thread on the side opposite the pins. Work two rows at a time, position a pin at the end of each row, and tie off the pair of threads. Continue this way until all threads are tied off in pairs.

Lightly steam the pleats to set them. Hold the iron just above the fabric until the fabric is slightly damp. Let the piece cool and dry before removing the pins.

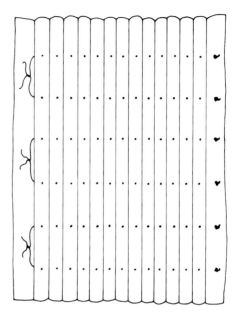

◄ Adjust the gathering threads so the pleated piece is exactly the same width top to bottom, then tie them off in pairs.

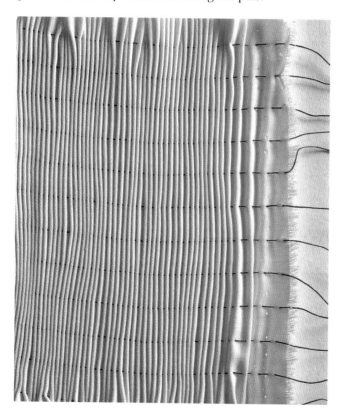

FINISHING THE SMOCKING

When the smocking has been worked, stitch along the upper and lower seamlines with a machine basting stitch. Remove the gathering threads. Pull the threads out carefully in case they are caught in any of the stitching. Pin the piece to the ironing board as before, wrong side up. Steam the piece and allow it to dry pinned in place.

2 Designing with Smocking

With simple combinations of just the basic smocking stitches it is possible to create hundreds of fascinating patterns and original designs. When you begin to experiment with threads and colors, to add beads or embroidery, and to try out unlikely fabrics, the design potential is nearly limitless.

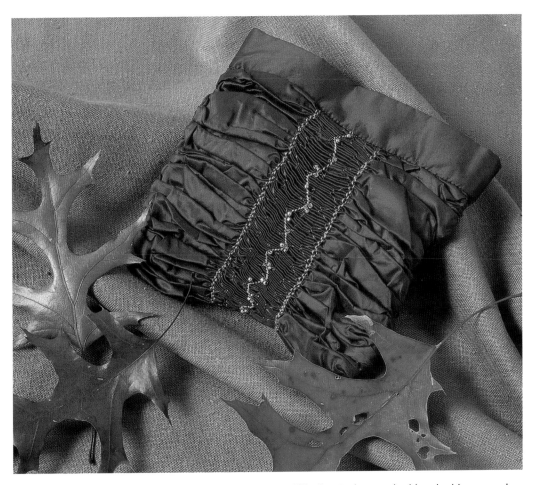

On a small evening bag (described in detail on page 73), the single smocked band adds textural interest and provides a ground for just the right amount of embellishment.

Planning a Design

SMOCKING ON A GARMENT or other piece can be purely decorative or can function as it did in the centuries-old garments, controlling the fabric fullness. The smocking might be barely visible, or it can be the focal point of a garment or project.

Even the simplest smocking pattern, worked over just a small area of a garment or other piece, can be very beautiful and require little time to do. Because it is a three-dimensional technique, smocking can be more effective than flat embroidery alone.

▶ A simple wave stitch pattern is worked vertically in two colors to accent the sleeve. The design is back-smocked so the sleeve will fit closely at the wrist and lower arm.

▼ Wave stitch with a single, very long diagonal stitch is combined with cables to create a striking and unusual pattern. It is worked with variegated silk floss in hues that blend with those of the silk fabric.

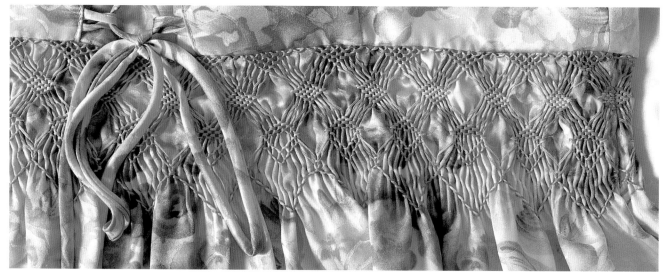

The stitches themselves can be altered, exaggerated, condensed, and manipulated in all sorts of ways. Cable and outline stitches can be used to create shapes. Wave stitches are well-suited to all kinds of geometric patterns; vandyke stitches shape readily into hearts.

Whatever form your smocking design will take, consider the qualities of the stitches you plan to incorporate. Does the project require elasticity in the area that will be smocked? Will the design be small and delicate, or should bold stitch patterns be used? Will the design require backsmocking? Think about the overall project as you decide upon the stitch design you would like to use.

► A delicate smocking pattern was chosen to control the fullness on the sleeve of a summery linen blouse.

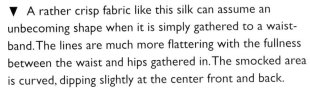

▼ A rather crisp fabric like this silk can assume an unbecoming shape when it is simply gathered to a waistband. The lines are much more flattering with the fullness between the waist and hips gathered in. The smocked area is curved, dipping slightly at the center front and back.

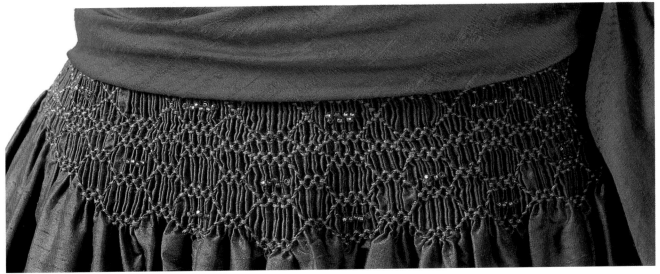

When you begin to work with unfamiliar stitches, threads, or fabrics, make a small sampler first to see how the combination strikes you. Fabrics take to pleating in different ways. The same stitch may not look the same on two different fabrics. One thread can work up differently than another. Keep all your stitch samples; they will provide good reference material for future designs.

Be objective about your designs. If you find the results are not what you had hoped, move on. The next try will be more successful. Remember that with smocking, as with most designing, less is often best. Stop short of adding too many stitches or colors to a single project—save some for the next one.

▲ Even for the pros, a sampler usually precedes the final project design. This one was worked up to test stitch combinations for some of the ornaments shown on page 78.

◄ Smocking makes an elegant alternative to the predictable gathers at the attachment points of a tie belt on a girl's dress.

Experiments with Threads and Fabrics

THE SAME STITCH pattern can assume a whole new personality when it is worked in a different thread. Two or three strands of cotton floss will always produce pleasant results, but it's fun to experiment. A basic wave stitch worked in colored metallic thread makes a bold statement; with a single strand of silk the effect is very subtle. Fine thread the color and sheen of the fabric renders the stitch nearly invisible, allowing the fabric texture the starring role in the design.

Generally, the thread should be reasonably compatible with the fabric, the size of the smocked area, and the pattern. Pearl cotton wouldn't be the best choice for a small wave pattern on a child's dress made of sheer silk, for example. Most combinations, though, are worth at least a try. The effect may not be just what you want for the current project, but it may be perfect for the next one.

▼ Metallic thread in a slightly different shade provides a dramatic accent well-suited to the rich velvet of an evening jacket.

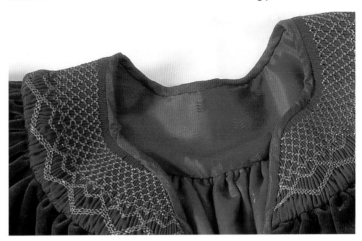

▲ The combination of a carefully chosen thread color and strong smocking design add just the right accent to the printed fabric.

▲ A narrow band of smocking, worked in variegated silk floss, complements the fabric's soft color without overwhelming it.

Contrasting thread emphasizes the stitching. Thread of a different color than the fabric, or thread with a different texture and sheen, will highlight the stitch pattern. If the thread matches the fabric, the eye is more likely to notice the textural effect of the smocked area, or the shaping created by the smocking.

For patterned fabric, a harmonious design just about always results when the smocking pattern includes two or more colors that appear in the fabric. It is effective, too, to add a solid-colored accent—a collar on a dress or blouse to go with a skirt—and smock it using the colors from the patterned fabric.

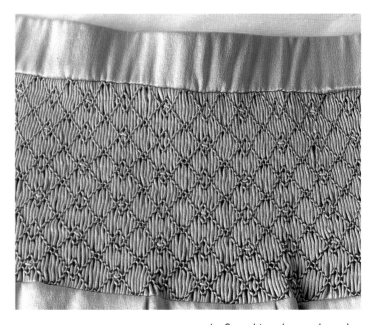

▲ Smocking shapes the yoke of a pleated silk charmeuse skirt so it fits smoothly around the hips. Worked in matching thread, the overall effect is one of texture.

◄ Even denim can be smocked if a little common sense goes into the design. This fabric is light in weight, and fine thread was used for the smocking to avoid creating a heavy look in an inappropriate place. The smocked area is a separate yoke, with the smocking worked tightly and backsmocked along all the gathering lines. The result is less bulk around the hips than would be the case if the fabric were pleated onto the waistband.

Fabric qualities, too, affect the overall look of the smocking. Cotton lawn pleats up tightly into smooth folds. Dupion silk, a favorite of many of the designers whose work is included in this book, has an irregular surface, the characteristic sheen of silk, and a crispness that produces a wonderful texture when it is pleated and stitched. As the photos on page 33 show, the two can be smocked in the same design with very different results.

Rather soft fabrics, fine to medium in weight, are the easiest to work with, especially if you are a relatively inexperienced smocker. Once you feel comfortable with the stitches and can keep the stitch tension nice and even, do try using some non-traditional fabrics—you may create some unique effects.

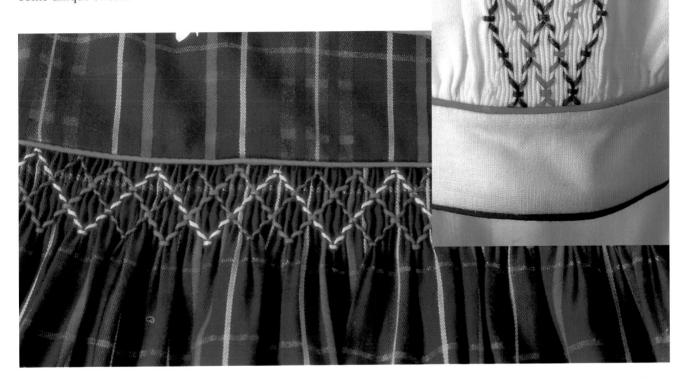

▲ At the waistline of a girl's jumper, bright colors from the plaid were used for the smocking. It was stitched with four strands of floss to give the smocking the same weight as the fabric pattern. The design is repeated on the blouse sleeve, with the cuff edged in piping of the same colors.

Mixing Metaphors

SMOCKING IS, in the first place, a fabric manipulation technique, a means of changing the surface appearance of the material. All sorts of intriguing effects are created when smocking is used in conjunction with other stitching techniques that alter the fabric's texture.

▲ The three-dimensional quality of trapunto (stuffed quilting) provides a pleasant contrast to the texture of the pleated and smocked areas of this art piece. The piece is shown in its entirety on page 109.

Can you find the smocking on the jacket at right? In a collage of fabric manipulation techniques, smocking provides just one element of the overall design. It blends perfectly with outline quilting, appliqué, and stitch-and-slash techniques. (Stitch-and-slash involves sewing parallel lines or a grid pattern through layered fabrics, then cutting through the upper layers between stitching lines to expose the bottom layer.)

▲ Designer Nellie Durand titled her award-winning jacket Looking for Elvis. His portrait, on fabric, is appliquéd along one sleeve and inside a pocket.

◄ The smocked section has no stitching at all on the right side. It is backsmocked with trellis stitch to give the pleats a wavy texture.

A favorite dropped-waist dress pattern, made up in soft corduroy, offers a great opportunity to blend fabric techniques and create a unique design. For the front inset, strips of the same corduroy were sewn into tubes then interwoven to create a latticework panel. The sleeve was widened to allow for a smocked panel (see page 97) that repeats the lines and colors of the design on the front.

◄ ▲ On a woman's dress, smocking on the sleeve complements the woven latticework design on the front, echoing colors and patterns. The wave stitch pattern is worked vertically, and backsmocked so the sleeve will fit closely at the wrist and lower arm.

Smocking, a form of trapunto, and tied quilting collaborate in the comforter shown below. The evenly striped pattern of the handwoven Indian silk allowed for smocking directly onto the fabric without pre-pleating the fabric, which would have been a life's work in itself.

Long, loose cable stitches were worked on the wrong side of the top section perpendicular to the stripes. For ease in handling, the smocking was done a section at a time rather than in rows the length of the piece. A fat strand of yarn was then drawn under the cable rows to fill each pleat.

For the backing, a flat piece of the same fabric was cut approximately 2 inches (5 cm) larger all around than the top. The edges were folded up around the top, turned under, and hemmed in place to create a smooth border. The top and backing were tied together at regular intervals with fine yarn.

▼ Backsmocking provided a framework for the filling in a silk comforter that's as functional as it is elegant.

Stitches and Techniques

For all its variety, traditional smocking involves relatively few different stitches, and none of them are difficult to work. The creative excitement of smocking comes with experimentation: trying out stitch combinations, combinations of stitches and fabrics, and combinations of stitches and threads.

Stitching Basics

IF YOU ARE a beginning smocker, it is a good idea to work up a small sampler to familiarize yourself with the characteristics of the different stitches and to help you get a feel for the best tension to use when working each one. A successful sampler can be displayed on a wall or used as a pillow front. At worst, you will have a visual reference for future project planning.

Count the number of pleats across the piece as you plan a design. Mark the center pleat or space so you can center the design and know where it the pattern repeat it will begin and end.

Unlike embroidery, smocking begins with a firmly knotted thread behind the first pleat. For most stitches, the needle is brought through to the right side of the fabric at the left side e of the first pleat. To tie off a thread, take several small back stitches on the back of a pleat. Don't knot the thread through two adjacent pleats; that can spoil the appearance of the design.

Stem, outline, and cable stitches can be worked right along a gathering line. Stitches with height are worked with the gathering threads serving to determine high and low points of each stitch sequence.

Most stitches are worked from left to right (if you are left handed, work from right to left). The vandyke stitch is worked from right to left, and the feather stitch is easier to work with the pleats held horizontally.

Whether the thread is above or below the needle as a stitch is taken makes all the difference in the appearance of a stitch. Generally speaking, keep the thread below the needle to make the level stitch at the bottom of a wave or diamond pattern and when working upward. Keep it above the needle for the level stitch at the top and when working downward.

To form a stitch, insert the needle into a pleat, usually from right to left, about one-third of the way down its depth and bring it out the other side at the same depth. If stitches are made too close to the surface, the pleats will pull apart when the gathering threads are removed. If they are too close to the valleys between pleats, stitching is difficult and the pleats will be distorted.

In traditional work, the pleats of a smocked piece should sit neatly side by side without gaps (unless you want gaps), but not be held so tightly together that the roundness is lost. On the other hand, purposeful distortion of the pleats is great fun and can produce interesting results.

Smocking Stitches

STITCH NOMENCLATURE CAN be confusing. Most stitches are known by more than one name, and some names apply to more than one stitch. Perhaps stitches should be given internationally recognizable Latin names, like plants. The name by which you know a stitch doesn't matter as long as you know which to use to achieve the effect you want.

▶ Remarkably diverse effects can be achieved with a few uncomplicated smocking stitches.

Stem Stitch and Outline Stitch

THESE TWO STITCHES differ only in the way the thread is held during the stitching, and the names are used interchangeably. Stem stitch is also known as *rope stitch*. Stem and outline stitches are firm, with little stretch, making them popular for holding pleats neatly in place along the upper and lower gathering threads of a smocked area. They also are used, as the names suggest, to define an area of picture smocking as shown on page 32.

Each stem stitch slants downward from left to right.

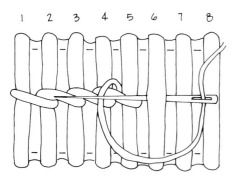

Begin by bringing the needle out at the left side of the left pleat. With the thread held below the needle, take a stitch from right to left through the second pleat, at the same level.

Make the next stitch from left to right through the third pleat.

Continue stitching through each pleat in this way across the row.

The outline stitch is made in the same way, but with the thread held above. This causes the stitches to slant upward from left to right.

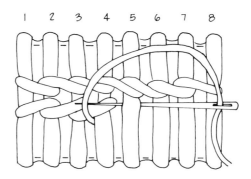

A row of stem stitch with a row of outline stitch worked closely below is sometimes called, collectively, *mock chain* or *wheat stitch*.

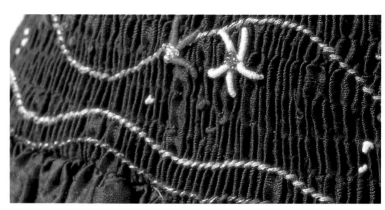

► A simple yet sophisticated design is created with just outline stitch and bullion accents.

Cable Stitch

LIKE STEM AND outline stitches, cable is worked in a straight horizontal line across the pleats. It is a firm stitch, although slightly less so than stem and outline. It is the stitch most often used for backsmocking, where just a little elasticity is desirable.

Cable stitch is worked the same way as outline or stem stitch, but the thread is held alternately above then below the needle to give the finished line of stitching a different appearance, somewhat like brickwork.

Bring the needle up at the left side of the left pleat.

With the thread below and the needle level, take a stitch from right to left through the second pleat. (A)

Hold the thread above and take a second stitch from right to left through the third pleat at the same level. (B)

Hold the thread below again, and stitch through the fourth pleat. Alternate these steps to continue across the row.

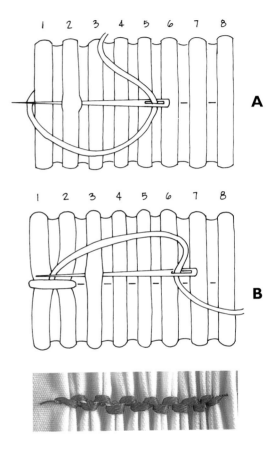

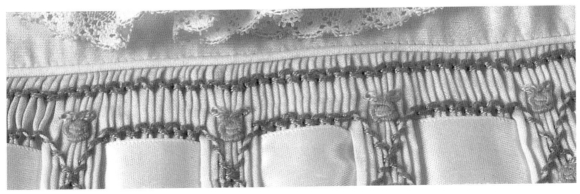

▲ A single row of cable stitch along the upper gathering line holds the pleats in place. As a decorative stitch, it is effective for highlighting another stitch pattern or design area.

DOUBLE CABLES AND STACKED CABLES

Two rows of cable worked closely together constitute a double cable. For parallel double cables, the second row is a reverse of the first: when the thread is held below the needle for the first stitch of the first row, it should be held above for the first stitch of the second row to give the cables a stacked appearance.

► Stacked cables worked with four strands of floss or with heavier thread produce a solid area of color. Outline stitch in a contrasting color defines the design.

When the second row is worked exactly as the first, the pattern is referred to as *alternating cable.*

Stacked cables are multiple rows of either parallel or alternating cable stitch. Stacked cables are used when solid areas of color are desired, as with picture smocking (described on page 45).

CABLE FLOWERETTE

A simple and effective motif results from working the first two or three stitches of two rows of double cables. The design looks like a small embroidered satin stitch pattern, but the stitches are actually smocking stitches, worked through the pleats. They are a nice accent when worked in a contrasting color.

Wave Stitches

THESE ARE ALSO known as *trellis*, *chevron*, and *diamond stitches*, depending upon the pattern that develops when multiple rows are worked. They comprise the largest and most versatile group of stitches used for smocking, and can be varied in countless ways.

A wave stitch is essentially a series of cable stitches, each connecting two pleats. Wave stitches can be worked to span the distance between two gathering threads, or half that height. They can be regular and even, or can create a random zigzag pattern across the pleats. Wave and trellis stitches can be very elastic or slightly so, depending upon the height of the pattern repeat and the number of stitches making up each sequence.

The diagonal line between top and bottom of the stitch sequence may consist of a single stitch, or several. With more stitches, of course, more pleats will be involved in each pattern repeat.

A single row of wave stitch produces a zigzag pattern. The trellis pattern results when two or more rows are worked parallel to one another. When the stitch sequence is worked in multiples of two rows with the stitch direction alternating, a pattern of diamonds or chevrons is created across the pleats.

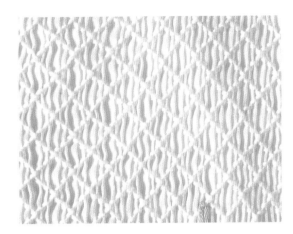

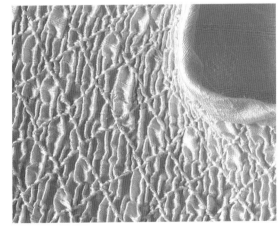

◀ Two entirely
◀ different surface textures are created by the same wave stitch. The dress below is dupion silk, the one above is cotton batiste.

FULL-SPACE WAVE

This version is called a *two-step wave*, or *trellis*. There is a stitch midway between the upper and lower level stitches of the wave. It extends from one gathering line to the next.

Bring the needle out at the left side of the first pleat on the lower line of gathering. With the thread below, take a stitch from right to left through the second pleat at the same level. (A)

Keeping the thread below, make the next stitch halfway between the gathering rows through the third pleat. (B)

At the upper gathering line, keep the thread below and make a stitch, right to left, through the fourth pleat. (C)

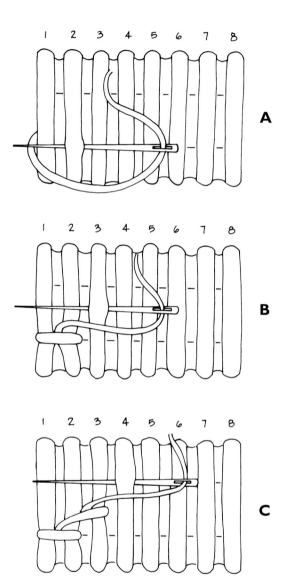

A

B

C

With the thread above the needle, make a stitch at the same level through the fifth pleat. (D)

Now work downward. Keeping the thread above, take a stitch through the sixth pleat at the midway point with the needle angled slightly downward. (E)

Hold the thread above the needle and take a stitch through the seventh pleat, along the lower gathering line.

The bottom level stitch is the last stitch of this sequence and the first of the next. With the thread below, take a stitch through the eighth pleat at the same level.

For a diamond or lattice pattern, start the second row with a level stitch just under the first stitch of the row above. Work downward first, then upward.

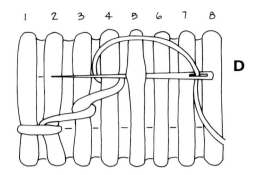

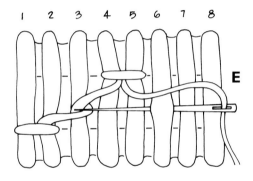

HALF-SPACE WAVE

Also called the *baby wave*, this stitch is often worked between a gathering row and a point midway between that row and the next one above or below. A single diagonal stitch connects the upper and lower level stitches.

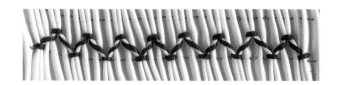

It might be helpful for a beginner to mark the halfway point between two rows of gathering by running a single strand of embroidery floss across the row through the backs of the pleats.

This stitch can also be worked to cover the entire distance between two gathering lines.

Bring the needle out at the left side of the first pleat at the bottom point of the wave. With the thread below, take a level stitch from right to left through the second pleat. (A)

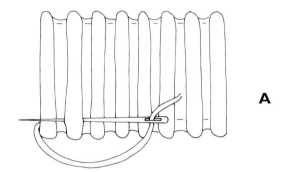

A

At the top point of the pattern, hold the thread below the needle and take a level stitch, right to left, through the third pleat.

With the thread above the needle, make a second stitch at the same level through the fourth pleat. (B)

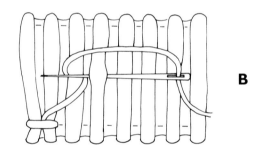

B

Hold the thread above the needle and take a stitch through the fifth pleat, level with the first stitch. (C)

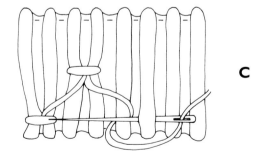

C

The bottom stitch is the last stitch of this sequence and the first of the next. With the thread below, take a stitch through the sixth pleat at the same level as the previous stitch.

LARGE WAVE

This is the basic wave with an additional stitch on each diagonal line. It is worked in the same way, but with the stitches between the top and bottom taken one-third of the way up or down the appropriate pleats. Each stitch sequence will cover two additional pleats.

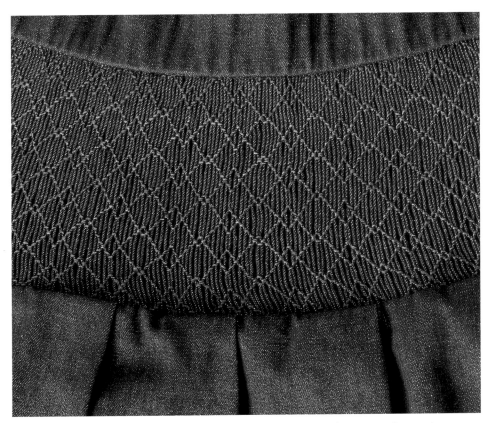

▲ Rows of large wave stitch create a diamond pattern and can incorporate almost any number of stitches along the diagonal line. In this one, worked with a strand each of metallic green and red, larger diamonds overlap to create a pattern of smaller ones.

Vandyke Stitch

THIS STITCH LOOKS a bit like the small wave, but it affects the pleats differently. When a second row is worked in the reverse direction, the spaces between pleats appear almost square. It is worked from right to left, but the needle is still inserted right to left to form the stitches.

Begin by bringing the needle up at the left of the second pleat from the right on the upper line of the stitch. With the thread above, make a level stitch through the first and second pleats. (A)

Keeping the thread above, take a stitch through the second and third pleats on the lower line. (B)

With the thread below, work a stitch through the third and fourth pleats on the upper line. Continue this way, with each pleat included in both an upper and a lower stitch. (C)

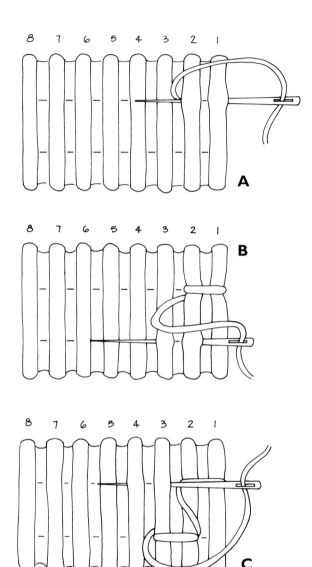

► Vandyke is a good stitch choice for counterchange, or direct, smocking.

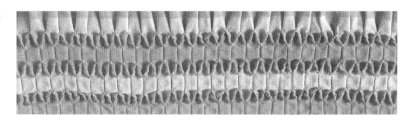

Honeycomb Stitch

ALSO CALLED *spot honeycomb*, this stitch is very elastic, and requires less fabric than other stitches. It can be worked on checked or dotted fabric without pre-pleating.

Honeycomb stitch creates wonderful surface texture. With matching thread, the stitches are barely visible. Contrasting thread will produce small spots of color, but be sure the diagonal stitches on the back will not show through.

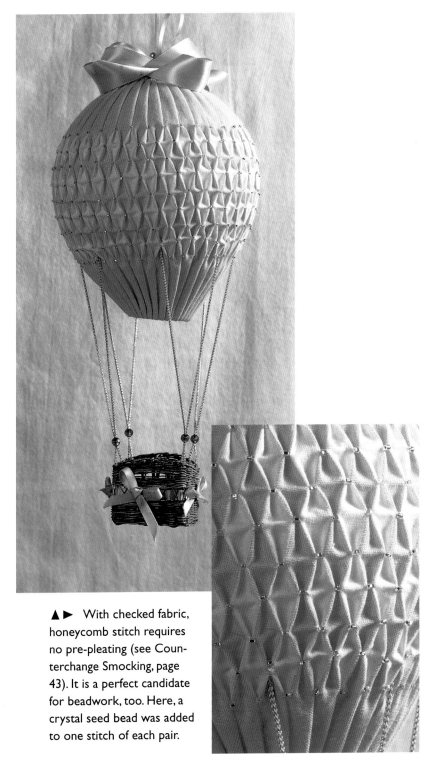

▲ ▶ With checked fabric, honeycomb stitch requires no pre-pleating (see Counterchange Smocking, page 43). It is a perfect candidate for beadwork, too. Here, a crystal seed bead was added to one stitch of each pair.

Bring the needle out at the left side of the first pleat on the upper gathering line of the pattern. With the thread above, take a level stitch from right to left through the second and first pleats, and snug them together. (A)

Keeping the thread above, insert the needle on the right side of the second pleat again. On the back, aim it down to the lower gathering line and bring it out at the left side of the second pleat. (B)

With the thread below, take a stitch from right to left through the third and second pleats. (C)

Insert the needle into the right side of the third pleat again, and aim it upward. Bring it out at the upper line on the left side of the third pleat. (D)

Continue the row this way. For the second stitch of each pair, insert the needle close enough to the previous stitch that the two will lie neatly one on top of the other. Start the second row as the first to keep the pattern consistent.

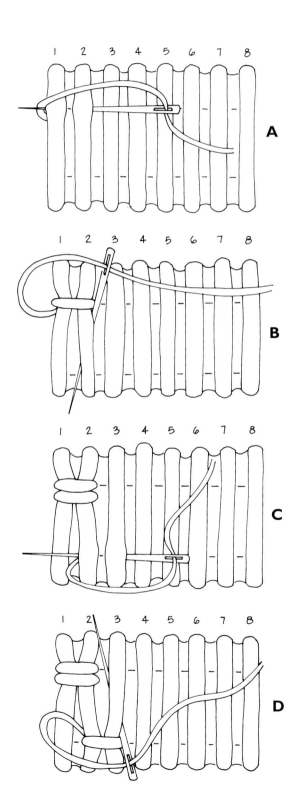

SURFACE HONEYCOMB

In a way, surface honeycomb is the reverse of honeycomb stitch, in that the diagonal stitches connecting the satin stitch pairs are on the front of the work. It looks very much like the small wave stitch, but produces a different surface texture.

Bring the needle out on the left side of the first pleat at the upper gathering line. With the thread above the needle, take a stitch from right to left through the second pleat. (A)

Keeping the thread above, take another stitch through the second pleat along the lower gathering line. (B)

With the thread below, take a stitch through the third pleat at the same level. (C)

Keep the thread below, and take another stitch through the third pleat on the upper gathering line. Continue along the row in this way. (D)

If alternate rows are stitched in the opposite way, with the first stitch worked from the lower to the upper gathering line, a diamond pattern will result.

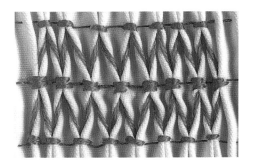

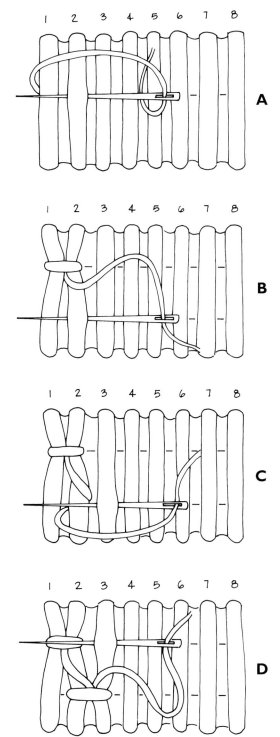

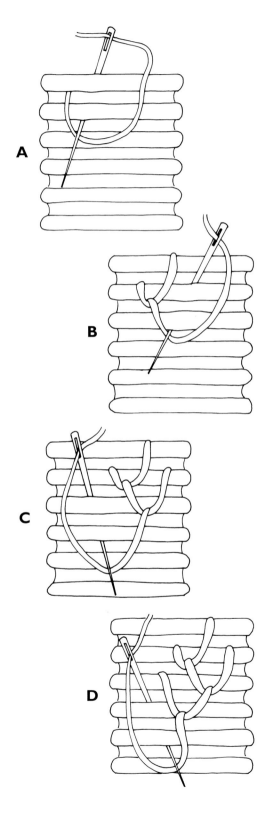

Feather Stitch

A POPULAR EMBROIDERY stitch, feather stitch works just as well for smocking. This stitch has little elasticity; take care to keep the stitch tension even so the pleats are not drawn up too tightly. It is easiest to work feather stitch with the pleated fabric turned horizontally, with the right edge upward. The pattern can be centered over a gathering line or worked between two of them.

Bring the needle up at the underside of the top pleat. Hold the thread down and slightly to the right, and take a stitch downward through the first and second pleats. Bring the needle out over the thread to form a loop. (A)

Work the next stitch in the same way, slightly to the right, through the second and third pleats. (B)

Work the next stitch to the left, in the same way, through the third and fourth pleats. (C)

Make another stitch to the left through the fourth and fifth pleats. Repeat the sequence along the row. (D)

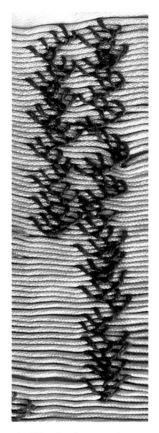

▲ The feather stitch on this sampler was worked with four steps each direction.

Special Smocking Techniques

SOME OF THESE stitches are less often used in "traditional" smocking, but have characteristics that render them most useful in certain situations. Here, too, are techniques, traditional and less so, for putting the stitches together.

Backsmocking

STITCHING ON THE back of the smocked piece keeps the pleats together neatly when the chosen design is sparse or too elastic to do so. Backsmocking (*also called reverse smocking*) is especially important with picture smocking, where the appearance of the design depends upon the pleats being firmly together.

Functional backsmocking is most often done with cable stitch. Cable has a slight bit of stretch, is fast to work, and won't show through to the right side of the piece. Outline or stem stitch can be used instead, but these tend to bias the fabric.

Work backsmocking with one or two strands of floss in a color to match the fabric. Stitch along the gathering lines, keeping the tension even. Stitch into just the upper edge of each pleat so the stitches won't be visible on the right side of the work.

If the smocking design includes picture smocking or a pattern that will involve color changes, it is easier to backsmock before working the decorative smocking to avoid working over knots.

▲ A precise geometric pattern looks best with the pleats tightly aligned. Backsmocking was worked along all the gathering lines to hold the pleats together.

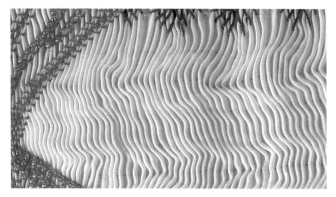

▲ In this detail from the sampler on page 29, backsmocking manipulates the pleats to create a wonderful rippled pattern on the surface.

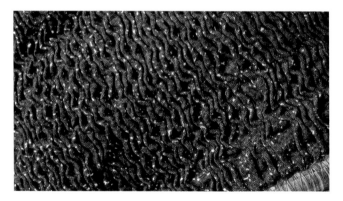

▲ Vandyke stitch was used for backsmocking to create texture on the right side of the piece.

Backsmocking, used decoratively, can be an effective part of an overall design. Although the stitches won't be visible on the right side, the resulting surface texture will be. For example, a pleated section of fabric might feature just a small central design on the right side, and be backsmocked with wave stitch to create an overall pattern across the pleated area.

Backsmocking on its own is a very versatile fabric manipulation technique, too. All kinds of textural effects are possible, and experimentation with different stitches and fabrics will produce all sorts of surprises.

◄ On the back of the bird shown on pages 106 and 107 there is no stitching at all on the right side. Backsmocking worked in vandyke stitch on the stiff silk produces an appropriately feathery texture.

Picture Smocking

SMALL MOTIFS, or pictures, can be incorporated into a smocking design with cable stitches worked closely together to completely cover the defined area. Two or more colors can be used to add realism or dimension.

Picture smocking is usually worked with three, or even four, strands of floss to give solid coverage of the area. Stitches are best worked slightly deeper into the pleat, the needle inserted half to two-thirds of the way down the pleat's depth. Stitch tension should be slightly looser, and very consistent. To work stitches over a small area like this, turn the work upside down to stitch the alternate rows.

Because of the nature of the cable stitch, square and triangular shapes are especially well-suited to picture smocking and a good choice for first design attempts. Outline stitch can be worked around the perimeter of a motif to smooth things out when a rounded line is called for (see the photo on page 32).

► The diagonal sides of a watermelon slice make it a good candidate for picture smocking; a triangular shape is easy to achieve with rows of cable stitch. "Seeds" were embroidered on top after the smocking was finished.

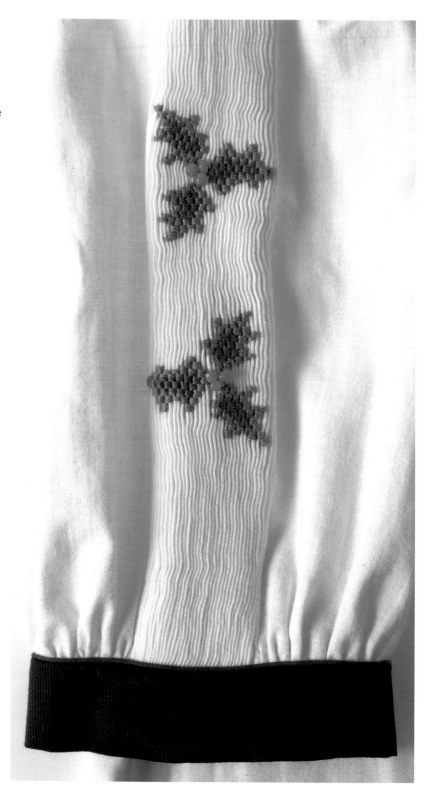

► A subtle color change around the edges adds a three-dimensional quality to the holly leaves.

Picture smocking designs should be backsmocked. The pleats will be kept firmly together so the design appears crisp and neat.

When two or more colors are used for a motif, it is easiest to keep to a single color for each row. When a design does call for a second color in a row, continue to work a row of stitching at a time as usual rather than skipping around to accommodate the color changes. Work with the first color until you reach the point where the color change occurs. Thread a second needle with the second color, and continue on! Finish the first color with a stitch through to the right side of the pleat, and bring the second color through on the left side.

Vertical Smocking

SOME DESIGNS ARE easier to work vertically—up and down the pleats—rather than in horizontal rows. Vertical smocking can be done to accommodate a particular arrangement of colors, as in the design at right, or just as a design feature, as shown below.

Wave, or trellis, stitch adapts to vertical rows nicely. The pattern is simply angled left or right where it would change upward or downward when worked across a horizontal row. The only difference is that the needle exits from a different pleat than it would if the stitch were worked horizontally.

Work one leg of the zigzag stitch to the point where it is to change direction. Make a cable stitch while positioning the thread on the side of the needle toward the previous stitch. Be sure the thread exits the cable on the side that the row is traveling toward.

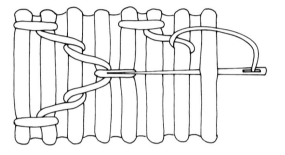

▲ Vertical lines of stitching with four strands of floss in crayon colors create a bold diamond pattern.

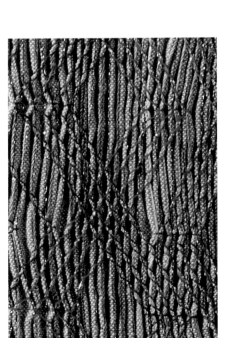

◀ In this art piece (shown in its entirety on page 105) very fine metallic thread was used to stitch an overall vertical zigzag pattern.

Counterchange Smocking

ALSO KNOWN AS *direct smocking*, counterchange is quick and fun to work. With checked or striped fabric, the fabric pattern serves as a guide for placement of the stitches and the fabric need not be pleated before stitching.

► Counterchange smocking was worked on a ¼-inch (.7-cm) checked gingham in vandyke stitch. The stitch pattern produces horizontal stripes in the finished piece.

Counterchange requires less fabric than methods that call for pre-pleated fabric. Usually about twice the planned finished width of the piece is enough. Honeycomb and vandyke stitches are often used for direct smocking. Others will work, too, and can provide an interesting ground for experimentation.

Choose a fabric with evenly spaced small-to medium-sized checks, or stripes. Be sure the pattern is woven into the fabric, not printed on it. Printed patterns usually do not follow the fabric grainline and will result in a skewed piece of smocking. For striped fabrics, mark horizontal guidelines at right angles to the stripes, ⅜ to ½ inch (1 to 1.3 cm) apart.

Counterchange smocking is a great fabric manipulation technique. It is possible to plan the stitching to obscure certain colors in a checked or striped pattern while emphasizing others, creating all sorts of exciting effects.

To work counterchange, pick up a small "bite" of the fabric with each stitch. Plan so that each step of the stitch is worked at the same point of the check or stripe every time so the finished piece will exhibit an even color pattern.

◄ On the wrong side of the piece shown opposite, a different and equally interesting pattern appears.

Canadian Smocking

THIS TECHNIQUE, also called *North American smocking*, is actually more a fabric manipulation technique than classic smocking. There is almost no elasticity to the stitched fabric. Because the rich three-dimensional quality of the design would be lost if it were flattened, this pattern should be worked on fabric that won't crush easily. Cotton/polyester blends, wool challis, and dupion silk, for example, would be better choices than cotton batiste or handkerchief linen.

▶ Worked on firm polished cotton, the lattice pattern has a crisp look.

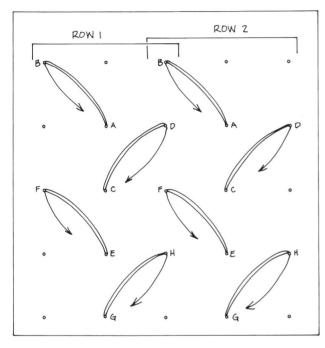

Working with a smaller grid, like that described below, also will help maintain the surface texture. A larger grid would work well with heavier fabrics like denim and velvet.

Mark the grid on the fabric wrong side. Space the dots approximately 1 inch (2.5 cm) apart.

The pattern is worked in vertical rows. Use a strong thread to match the fabric. Pick up dot A with a small right-to-left stitch. Pick up dot B in the same way and draw the two together. Take a stitch to hold the two firmly.

Take a stitch at C, keeping the thread and fabric flat between A/B and C. Pick up a stitch at D, then draw up the thread and stitch the two together as before. Continue this way down the row.

The illustrated pattern can be varied in many ways. Try, for example, changing the spacing of the dots, or adding space between vertical rows.

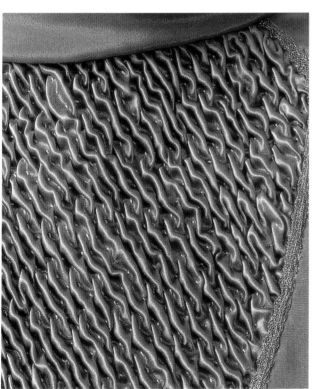

◄ A lattice design on soft polyester satin produces a smoother surface texture and will hold its shape beautifully.

4 Embellishments for Smocking

Smocking is, in itself, a wonderful form of embellishment. Its stitches and patterns adorn the pleated fabric as they hold the pleats in place. There are other techniques, though, that seem natural companions for smocked designs. The techniques shown in this chapter are especially compatible with smocking and are favored by the designers whose work is shown throughout these pages.

Piping

CORDED PIPING IS often used to define the seamline between a smocked section and flat fabric, or to finish an edge. It has a dimensional quality that echoes the shape of the pleats.

▲ Corded piping in the facing seamlines provides a nice contrast and complements the smocking pattern.

Fabric strips to cover the cord should be cut on the bias so the piping can be shaped neatly around curves and corners. If the piping will be used only in a straight seam, crossgrain strips will work fine.

Select cord of a diameter suitable for the garment or project. For most garments, fine to very fine cord will not overwhelm the smocking design. If the smocked pattern is a bold one, thicker cording might be used.

Cut fabric strips the diameter of the cord plus twice the seam allowance. If it is necessary to piece the strips, join them as shown, right sides together, and stitch them along the straight fabric grain.

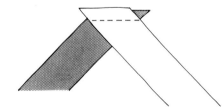

Wrap the fabric strip right side out around the cord and stitch close to the cord with a zipper or cording foot. To stitch it to the smocked piece, align the seamlines and raw edges, then stitch along the original stitching line of the piping. Clip the piping seam allowance to the stitching as necessary to go around curves and corners.

For smoother seamlines, flatten the seam allowances of the smocked section before attaching piping. Stitch around the seam allowance, close to the seamline, with a triple zigzag stitch or medium-length plain zigzag stitch.

◄ (opposite page) The piping at the waist and neckline is made with very fine cord to suit the proportions of a tiny christening dress.

Bias Bindings

SOMETIMES AN EDGE has no seam into which piping can be sewn. Bias bindings are a pretty alternative and make a nice finish at necklines and sleeves.

Cut fabric strip on the bias, four times the desired finished width and as long as needed, plus seam allowance at the ends. Press it in half lengthwise, right side out. Turn the raw edges in to the center crease, and press. Re-press the center fold so the edges are slightly mis-aligned, one side a bit short of the other.

Flatten the seam allowances of the smocked section as for piping. Trim the seam allowance, if necessary, so it is slightly narrower than that of the binding strip.

Fold under the beginning end of the strip. Pin it over the neckline edge, the shorter side of the strip on the outside of the garment. Stitch very close to the edge of the strip, catching the inner folded edge at the same time.

▲ Bias binding finishes a neckline neatly and secures the pleating at the neckline edge.

Beading

BEADS ADD ELEMENTS of sparkle and texture to smocking designs. Tiny crystal seed beads or pearls highlight a delicate pattern. Robust wooden beads might be used to complement a bold design on a decorative pillow.

▶ A simple cable and wave pattern takes on a distinctive character with the addition of a small pearl to each of the cable stitches.

Beading can be incorporated into the smocking itself, added to selected stitches as you go. Be sure to choose a thread and needle that will go through the bead easily if you work this way. Honeycomb stitch is a good one to combine with beading, as shown on page 39. Just the beads are visible; the stitches are hidden behind them.

Beads can be sewn on after the fact, too, which may be easier from a design standpoint. In this case, take care that the beading stitches don't restrict the stretch of the smocked area.

▲ Working up a small sampler is a good preface to any unexplored technique.

◄ The resulting ornament incorporates seed beads into its unusual design

▼ Diminutive pearls add just the right accent to a silk wedding gown. Delicate embroidery featuring bullion roses serves as a focal point at the neckline.

Woven Ribbon

MANY OF THE smocking stitches can serve as beading through which ribbon can be woven to create fascinating effects. Wave stitch works well for this technique; just allow a single diagonal stitch that is wide enough to accommodate the ribbon's width. Soft, pliable silk and rayon ribbons work better for weaving than the more resilient polyester and nylon.

Ribbon can also be interwoven through the smocking itself. Cut small vertical "buttonholes" in the valleys between pleats to weave the ribbon in and out. Space the slits between gathering rows at the desired intervals. If the piece is faced or lined and the fabric doesn't tend to ravel, it shouldn't be necessary to finish the cuts. Otherwise, use a small whipstitch to overcast the raw edges.

► Ribbon, woven in and out of cuts between the pleats, provides a pleasant contrast to the delicate embroidery on a child's dress. The smocking is a simple cable design, planned to emphasize the ribbon stripe. The roses are worked in bullion stitch.

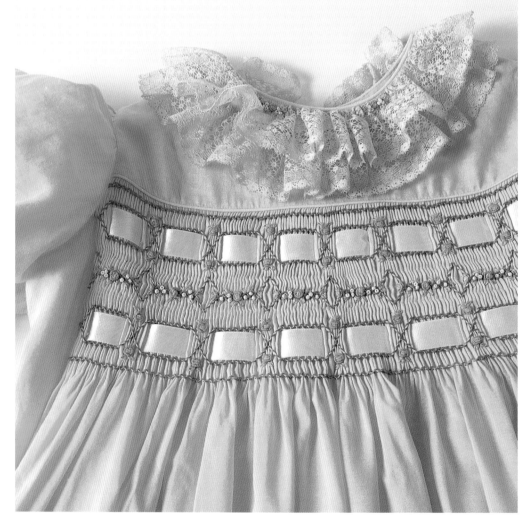

Embroidery Stitches

IN ADDITION TO those that make up the smocking itself, other traditional embroidery stitches can fill in a design with shapes, colors, and textures. Try incorporating threads in contrasting colors and of different thicknesses. Embroider with a strand of metallic thread if the smocking is all in cotton. Or use pearl cotton for French knots to give dimension to a flat piece.

Extra embroidery can serve a purpose, too. A variety of spider stitches, some with beads added, were used to close the ends of the ornaments shown on page 78.

When embroidery is worked over a completed piece of smocking, take care that the embroidery stitches don't constrict the pleats and diminish the elasticity of the smocking. To prevent such a worry, stitches worked over one or two pleats are a good choice.

There are hundreds of embroidery stitches that could be used with smocking patterns. The sampling given here includes stitches that are especially compatible with smocking and that are favorites of the designers whose work is shown in this book.

► Embroidered accents provide an interesting contrast to the simple diamond pattern of the smocking. A design of French knots, worked closely around a central bullion rose, add variety in texture and color.

FRENCH KNOTS

These are worked on a single pleat which makes them a good stitch for smocking. Randomly spaced, they add interesting texture. A single French knot can serve as the center of a bullion stitch or silk ribbon rose.

Bring the thread up through the top of a pleat. Wind the thread twice around the needle and hold securely with a fingernail. (A) Pivot the needle and insert it close to the base of the thread. (B) Secure the knot with a backstitch on the wrong side.

▲ French knots, each at the end of a "stem," decorate the bird's topknot. Clear glass beads echo the shape of the knots and add a little sparkle.

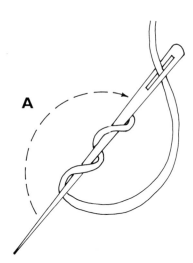

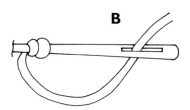

BULLION STITCH

Like a French knot, the bullion stitch can assume many forms depending upon the thread used to make it. It can be worked over two pleats.

Bring the needle up at the center of a pleat then insert it into the same or another pleat a short distance away, leaving a loop, then bring just the point back out at the original place. (A)

Wind the thread loop firmly around the needle a number of times until the coil is the same length as the space between the stitches. (B)

Hold the coil gently between finger and thumb, and pull the thread carefully through the coil. Continue pulling until the knot is against the fabric. Insert the needle again at the point where it entered the fabric the first time.(C)

BULLION ROSE

Work bullion stitches around a central French knot, always in the same direction, with the ends of the stitches overlapping slightly as with stem stitch. The flower will have more dimension if the coils are condensed toward the center and slightly looser at the perimeter.

A

B

C

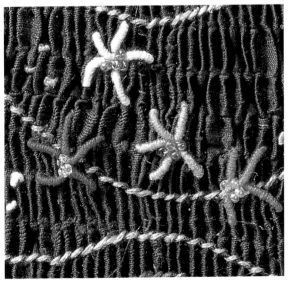

▶ Bullion stitches create the flowers, each with a crystal bead at the center.

SPIDER WEBS

With as many variations as there are embroiderers, spider webs of all descriptions are fun to do. Any form of the stitch is especially useful to close the ends of a tube-shaped piece of smocking, as for a round ornament.

The style illustrated below is an easy one to work. It calls for an odd number of stitches for the base; other variations can be worked with an even number of stitches.

Mark a circle on the fabric. Stitch across it several times from different points around the perimeter. Then take one more stitch from the edge to the center to make an uneven number of spokes.

Bring the needle up near the center between two stitches and weave it over, then under, around the circle. The first stitch of the second round should be under, and so on, so the weaving alternates.

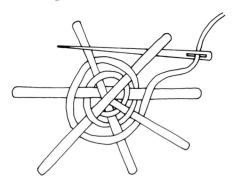

CHAIN STITCH

One of the most-used stitches, chain has been worked by nearly everyone with a needle and thread or a crochet hook. It is a simple stitch, yet can look like hundreds of different stitches when varied slightly or worked in an assortment of threads.

For the basic chain, bring the needle up at the beginning of the line of stitching and insert it at the same point, leaving a loop. (A)

Bring it up a short distance away, with the point over the thread loop. Continue this way to make the chain. (B)

The chain can be varied in many ways. Try twisting the thread loop. Widen the chain by leaving space between the upward and downward stitches in step A. Experiment with your own versions and favorite threads.

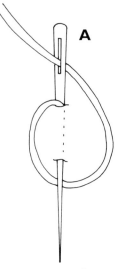

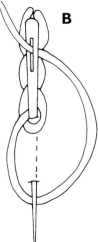

▲ The *Icicle Cape* is made of soft wool flannel, embellished with chain stitch and all its known variations. Smocking it is; however, there is pleating only at neckline. The pleats are completely covered by the embroidery, allowed to release over the shoulders and in back and front to give the cape its shape.

▲ On the back are still more chain stitch variations. The designer used every kind of floss, thread, and ribbon whose color met the specifications.

▲ A hint of sparkle is provided by water droplet accents embroidered with fine silver metallic thread.

Silk Ribbon

IF YOU HAVEN'T tried it, you will be pleasantly surprised to see the three-dimensional quality ribbon gives to even the most humble embroidery and smocking stitches. Silk ribbon designs are especially beautiful with smocked silk fabrics.

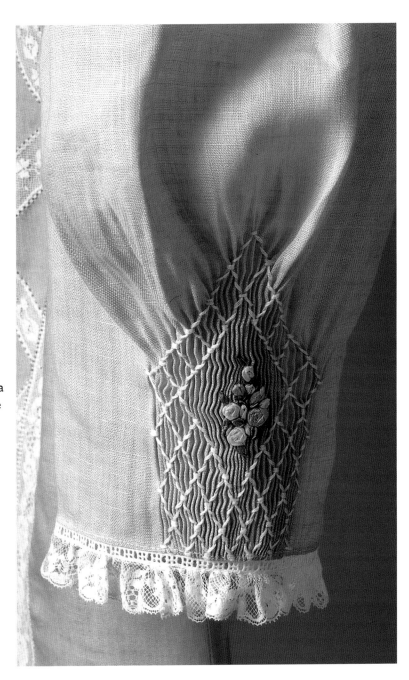

► Roses embroidered with silk ribbon create a focal point for the wave stitch pattern on the sleeve of a girl's dress.

Silk ribbon is available 2 mm, 4 mm, and 7 mm wide in a rainbow color range. A more limited color selection is available for wider ribbon widths. Working with silk ribbon is not difficult, but there are a few differences.

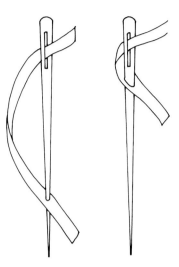

The ribbon does have width, so a needle with a longer eye may be necessary. Try a chenille needle if the crewel needle doesn't suit the ribbon. The ribbon can slip out of the needle's eye easily. To prevent this, lock it in place by stitching through the short end as shown in the drawing.

There is a tendency for the ribbon to twist and crease as you stitch. This can be made part of the design in some cases. Otherwise, it is just a matter of stitching more slowly and carefully than you do with floss. Keep the stitches a little looser.

▼ Silk ribbon roses are exactly the right accent for a dress of dupion silk. The simple wave stitch pattern allows the embroidery to dominate the design.

SMOCKING WITH RIBBON

The narrower ribbons work best for smocking. Any stitch pattern can be used, but those featuring longer diagonal stitches show the ribbon to its best advantage. Embroidered embellishments also worked with ribbon highlight the smocked designs nicely.

EMBROIDERED RIBBON ROSES

While it is most elegant, and looks very ornate, the stitches are simple ones. The size of the rose can be varied by using slightly longer stitches and/or wider ribbon. A French knot makes up the center, or a small pearl or bead can be used instead.

The simple rose illustrated below is worked with stem stitch—the same as that used for smocking. Allow the folds of the ribbon to lie at the outer edge of the circle. The spider web stitch, shown on page 62, also shapes a pretty rose.

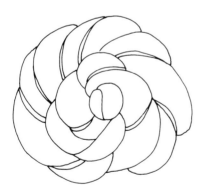

5

Designs for Smocking

Smocking is even more fun when your beautiful handwork
is displayed where others can enjoy and admire it too. In
this chapter is a selection of projects that feature smocking.
They are meant to show you ways in which smocking
can be used in your own designs, and to inspire
your own original smocked creations.

Christmas Tree Skirt

STRIPS OF RIBBON, smocked in red and green, add a very festive accent to a pieced tree skirt. Even after the packages are opened and gone, the space under the tree keeps its holiday look. Smocked ribbons on a smaller scale could make spectacular gift decorations or clever trim for Christmas stockings.

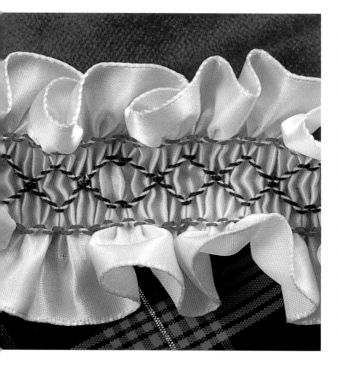

The upper skirt is made up of six alternating sections of taffeta and velvet. The backing is bright green taffeta, and there is a layer of thick batting between. Around the lower edge is a velvet ruffle 2½ inches (6.5 cm) wide with a 3½-inch (9-cm) eyelet ruffle beneath it. Narrow ribbon bows finish the lower edges of the smocked ribbons.

The finished skirt is approximately 48 inches (122 cm) in diameter. For lining and batting, you will need 1¼ yards (1.15 m) of 45-inch (115-cm) fabric. The matching ruffle requires a strip approximately 6 yards (5.5 m) in length and 3½ inches (9 cm) wide. For smocking, allow 8½ yards (7.35 m) of 2½-inch (6.5-cm) single-faced polyester ribbon. For the bows, allow 2½ yards (2.3 m) of narrow ribbon.

To make the skirt, fold the lining fabric in half, then in half again to form a square. Measure from the folded point with a tape measure to mark off the curved lower edge of the skirt, and cut along the marked line. Cut an inner circle approximately 7 inches (18 cm) in diameter.

From the lining, make a newspaper pattern for the sections of the upper skirt. Re-fold the lining into sixths and outline the shape. Add seam allowances at the straight edges.

Cut and assemble the upper skirt, leaving the piece open between the last two sections. Cut the lining and batting at the same point. Hem and gather the ruffles and baste them to one skirt section. Assemble the piece with right sides together and the ruffles between. Stitch around the inner and outer edges and along the straight edges, leaving an opening on one straight edge for turning.

Cut the wide ribbon into five equal lengths. Pleat three rows along the center of each piece. Pull the threads from the ends and hem them before drawing up the pleats. To maintain the ruffled edges, don't press the pleats before smocking. Work the smocking design of your choice. Tack the smocked pieces in place over the seamlines of the skirt and add a ribbon bow to each.

Handbags and Purses

ALWAYS USEFUL, and always welcome as gifts, little bags like these provide an opportunity to try new stitch patterns and threads on a small scale. These are made of dupion silk, a beautiful background fabric for smocked designs.

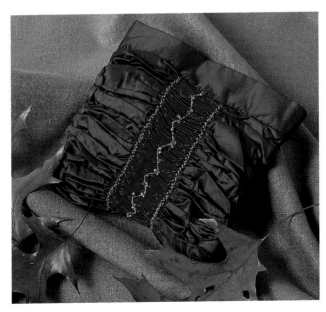

Bags for a Wedding Party

IVORY FOR THE bride and deep autumn red for the attendants, this elegant small bag is quick to smock and assemble. On the bride's bag, a wave pattern is worked with a single strand of variegated silk in pastel shades. The cable borders and central panel are stitched with a strand each of white silk and silver thread. The red attendant's bag has the same smocking design, worked in reds and silver.

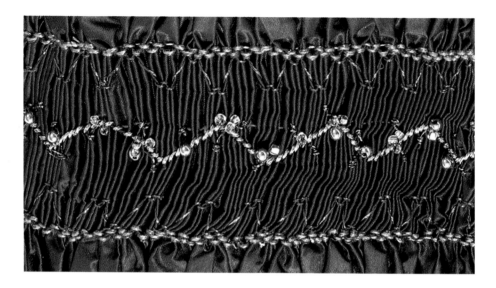

The finished bag is approximately 7 inches (18 cm) square. It is lined with lightweight silk, and closes with a silk-covered snap on the inner band.

To make the bag, cut silk for the outer bag 56 inches (142 cm) long and 15 inches (38 cm) wide. Cut lining 7 inches (18 cm) long and 15 inches (38 cm) wide. Cut a strip 3½ inches by 15 inches (9 cm by 38 cm) for the band.

For this design, the fabric is pleated on the lengthwise grain rather than across the grain as is usual. Pleat four rows along the center of the main fabric. Draw up the pleats and work the smocking.

Fold the piece in half, wrong side out, and sew the side seams with a machine basting stitch. Gather up the sides so they are the length of the smocked section. Tie off the threads.

Stitch the lining at the side seam and across the bottom. Place the lining in the bag and baste the two together around the upper edge.

Join the ends of the band. Press under the seam allowance on one edge. Stitch the other edge to the bag with right sides together. Fold the pressed edge to the inside, the fold over the stitching line, and stitch it in place by hand. Sew on the snap.

Made up in other fabrics, this bag could go anywhere. Chambray or linen, lightweight denim or brightly patterned cotton, almost any material would suit the design. Fabrics heavier than this silk will not pleat up as tightly and less length would be needed.

Change the design slightly and it can work equally well with heavy fabrics. Use a complementary material for the smocked panel and cut the sides as separate pieces. Remember to add seam allowances to all the pieces.

DAINTY DRAWSTRING BAG

A classic design dressed up, this eye-catching bag is approximately 10 inches (25 cm) high and 6 inches (15 cm) wide. It is smocked with red and silver metallic threads and accented with red seed beads. It is lined with lighter silk habutae and closes with ribbon drawstrings.

To make the bag, cut fabric 30 inches (76 cm) wide and 16 inches (40.5 cm) in length. Cut lining the same width and 13 inches (33 cm) long. You will also need 2 yards (2 m) of ¼-inch (.7 cm) ribbon.

Pleat the fabric, placing the first gathering line 6 inches (15 cm) from the top of the piece. For this bag five gathering rows were used.

Stitch the two short sides of the fabric together, leaving a ½-inch (1.3 cm) opening above the top gathering line. Work a buttonhole in the same position on the opposite side. Draw up the pleats and work the smocking. Remove the gathering threads. Stitch the bottom of the bag.

For the lining, stitch the short sides together. Stitch across the bottom, leaving an opening. Place the lining in the bag with right sides together. Stitch the bag to the lining and turn right side out through the lining opening. Stitch the opening.

On the inside of the bag, align the lining and bag seams. Stitch along the seam with machine basting through both layers. Draw up the threads to gather the bottom of the bag, and knot the threads securely.

Press the fold at the upper edge of the bag. For the ribbon casing, stitch around the bag just above and below the ends of the buttonhole. Thread the ribbons through the casing, one through one buttonhole and one through the other, and knot the ends.

This bag design is too good to keep just for formal occasions. It would be a simple matter to enlarge the pattern and make it of a bright cotton print to use as a beach bag, or in lightweight wool for everyday use.

SILKY DUFFLE

Its unusual shape makes this bag quite capacious despite its small size. The smocking design helps shape the bag; a tighter stitch pattern is used at the opening edge and tapers to a more sparsely stitched wave pattern below. In dupion silk as shown, the bag is lightweight and very graceful.

For the handles, narrow metallic ribbon is stitched to a wider length of ribbon to match the bag. The ends are stitched into the binding seam at the edge of the bag.

Cut a fabric rectangle for the body of the bag. In width it should be approximately four times as wide as the desired finished length (end to end) of the bag. In length, the piece should be the desired depth of the bag measured from one opening edge, over the smocking and around the bag to the other opening edge.

Pleat four to five rows at each end of the piece. Work smocking as desired, working downward from each edge (the edges will be at the opening of the bag).

Machine baste along the two long unsmocked edges. Gather each basting line tightly so that the smocked ends and gathered sides create a continuous circular edge.

Fold the piece with the gathers evenly arranged at each end. Mark positions for the ribbon handles. On the bag wrong side, position the ribbons, right sides against the bag wrong side and ends aligned with the bag edge. Baste them in place.

Cut a bias fabric strip for the edge binding. Cut the piece approximately four times the desired finished width of the binding and slightly longer than the bag raw edge to allow for overlap. Stitch it to the bag. (Detailed instructions are on page 54.)

If desired, sew a snap on the inside of the edge binding at the center of the opening, or sew one at the placement point of each ribbon. Silk-covered snaps make an especially elegant finish.

Smocking in the Round

IT'S MUCH SIMPLER than it looks! A small round ornament, whether to commemorate a holiday or to enjoy every day, is a quick project to make. The surface is so small that it provides a perfect way to explore possibilities with new stitches, new directions in pleating, new threads and fabrics, and new embellishments.

▲ FOREGROUND: Cinderella circles the sphere. The stitch is surface honeycomb; for the gowns it is worked in a variety of colors and embellished with crystal beads. Above and below, the finest metallic gold thread creates the borders. The faces are small satin stitches; the hair is strands of floss.
LEFT: a soft, subtle design is worked in pale lavender thread and pearl beads the same shade. REAR: spiraling stem stitch is accented with crystal beads.

These ornaments are made of lustrous silk charmeuse and crepe de chine, soft, pliable fabrics that respond well to pleating and smocking. Each is stitched and embellished in its own way, with generous beading for added shimmer.

For each ornament you will need a Styrofoam ball, fabric, threads, beads if you wish to add them, and ribbon or cord for the hanging loop.

Cut a piece of fabric half the circumference of the ball in length, and approximately four times the circumference in width. Fabrics differ in the amount by which they condense when pleated, so the width of the fabric needed will depend upon its thickness.

Pleat the fabric. Plan so the gathering rows are centered on the piece, with approximately ¼ inch (.7 cm) above and below the top and bottom rows.

Work the smocking. On each row stop one stitch before the last stitch. When the stitching is completed, trim away excess fabrics at the sides. Cut along the "valley" crease adjacent to the first and last pleats, taking care not to cut the gathering threads.

Sew the fabric into a tube, right sides together. Use thread to match the fabric and sew the cut edges together with small running stitches, close to the edge. Turn the tube right side out and work the last stitch of each row. Remove gathering threads except at the upper and lower rows.

Slip the ball into the tube. Trim the upper and lower edges to neaten them. Draw up the gathering threads.

Sew the hanger securely inside one end before closing the tube. The ends can be finished dozens of different ways. The spider web stitch, described on page 62, is attractive and is quick to work. Satin stitching all the way across the opening, and coils of beads are other alternatives to try. Threads from the end stitching can be left long and tied into tassels, as shown on two of the ornaments.

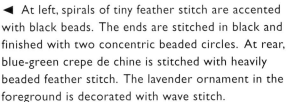

◄ At left, spirals of tiny feather stitch are accented with black beads. The ends are stitched in black and finished with two concentric beaded circles. At rear, blue-green crepe de chine is stitched with heavily beaded feather stitch. The lavender ornament in the foreground is decorated with wave stitch.

◄ At far left, deep purple silk is embellished with a wave stitch pattern in red and purple, each combined with fine metallic thread. A festive tassel combines all the threads used for the smocking. On the ornament at its right, outline stitch is worked in several colors and at varying angles to re-direct the pleats and create splendid textures in an ornament titled *The Pacific Ocean with Birds.* On the royal blue ball, gold silk thread adds luster to a spiraling feather stitch pattern, with gold-lined crystal beads to accent alternate stitches. Next, cable stitch in three colors decorates the peach ornament. Stitches in the same colors close the lower end and are left long to make the tassel. At right, the pale blue-green ornament features stem and feather stitches in a darker shade, highlighted with iridescent beads.

Smocking for Clothes

Smocked clothing is wearable art in one of its oldest and most appealing forms. The techniques are timeless, the stitches and patterns are every bit as fresh and lively with today's clothing styles. Whether used purely for decoration or to control fabric fullness, smocked accents still can give wearable art status to the simplest garment.

Smocking on Garments

THE EARLY SMOCKS—the garments from which the name of the technique derives—were boxy garments, often worn by farmers and laborers to protect the clothing. Fabric was a precious commodity, and garments were comprised of rectangular shapes cut so that no material was wasted. Fitting was done through the pleating and stitching. Embroidery stitch patterns were developed to gather in fullness in such a way that the gathered area had the necessary elasticity and allowed freedom of movement. Smocks exhibited this sort of stitching at the wrists and upper sleeve, and across the upper chest and back.

Smocking today is most often decorative in nature, and most often used on children's clothing. The trend toward a sleeker silhouette, both in women and in their clothing, has eliminated smocking to a large extent as a desirable form of embellishment except occasionally on nightwear. And men—who wore most of the original smocked garments—wear them now only under duress, and then only if they truly cherish the person who created them.

There are dozens of ways in which smocking can be incorporated into women's clothing designs with results that are both stylish and flattering. Smocking will, however, add bulk. The secret is to use smocking only in places where extra fullness is appropriate.

▲ Outline stitch worked in wavy lines, rather than straight across, defines a smocked area below the dress waistline without adding the appearance of extra width around the hips. The pattern is shown in detail on page 30.

Designing Smocked Clothing

THE GUIDELINES BELOW will help you plan a spectacular smocked garment.

- Make the garment the primary focus rather than the smocking. Smocking should contribute to the overall design of the garment but not overwhelm it. The smocked area can be functional, gathering in fabric fullness at certain points, or it can be strictly ornamental.

- Less is better. A single garment need not serve as a walking sampler of every known stitch and every available thread. There will be other garments—if the first one is a success. Smocking is far more effective when it is used judiciously.

- Choose fabric carefully. Lighter weight fabrics such as cotton lawn or voile, silk crepe de chine or charmeuse, and lightweight rayons are usually better choices for women's garments. If you are in doubt, pleat up a sample of the fabric to see the result. For novice smockers or sewers, cotton is easier to handle than slippery fabrics.

- Choose the pattern carefully. Many styles are designed in such a way that smocked areas can be added with ease; other patterns will work with some adjustment. Look at the possibilities on the following pages, then choose an adaptation that fits your level of skill and/or your spirit of adventure.

- Use an appropriate stitch pattern. A stitch design that reads as horizontal stripes probably wouldn't be the best choice around the waist or hips, for example, but could be attractive on a vertical inset in a sleeve. Consider the elasticity of the stitches, too, if the placement of the smocking will require that quality. Remember that diagonal stitches, such as the wave stitch family, stretch more than the straight outline and stem stitches.

- Make a sampler. It is especially important, with the amount of work and fabric a garment involves, to know in advance how your chosen combination of fabric, thread, stitches, and pleats will interact. Depending upon where the smocking will be placed, it can be important to know the extent to which the pleating and stitching will condense the fabric. There invariably are surprises. A few hours invested in the beginning can prevent weeks of work and a fortune in fabric ending up at the back of the closet.

There are several ways in which the necessary fullness can be added to a garment to accommodate smocking. Some patterns have the excess ease built in. With others, certain pieces can be widened and smocked up. In other cases, seams can be added and the smocking worked on an inset between two flat fabric sections. And smocking can simply be treated as appliqué, sewn onto the garment in a decorative fashion.

► The smocked area on this silk skirt is shaped for an attractive fit, curving downward from the sides to center front and back.

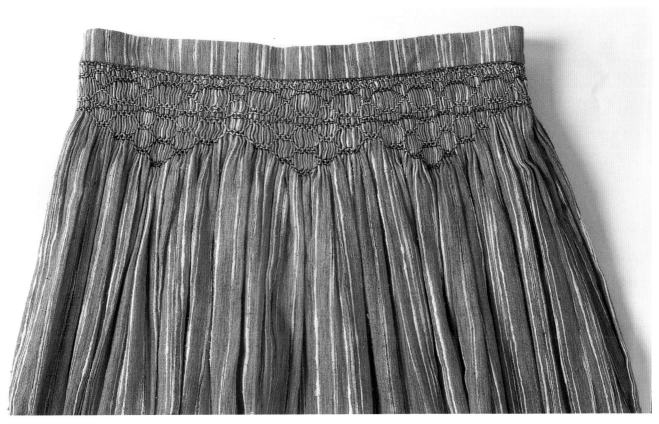

Working with Existing Patterns

FOR THOSE WHO are new to either smocking or pattern alteration, it is easiest to add smocking to a garment that already has sufficient ease to accommodate it. An oversized blouse, nightgown, or robe with the front and back gathered onto a yoke would be good patterns to try. A straight, generously sized dress or jumper would do nicely. A skirt that is gathered onto the waistband is a good candidate.

If smocking will be worked all the way around the garment, the pattern should not be a pull-on style, but should have a placket opening. The added smocking most likely will not have enough stretch to allow for pulling the garment over shoulders or hips. For tops, choose a pattern that has an opening in the yoke or that has a neck opening large enough to pull over the head. For a skirt, it is a simple matter to add a placket in the side seam.

▲ This designer avoided the illusion of a horizontal line across the hips by ending the smocking pattern with a deep wave stitch. The skirt is soft Indian silk, smocked with threads the colors of the fabric's stripes.

It is easiest, but not always possible, to avoid pleating fabric on which seams have been sewn. If the fabric will be pleated perpendicular to a seam, trim the seam allowances and press them open, then baste them in place until the fabric is pleated. Include them in the smocking stitching.

For a seam that is parallel to the pleating, try to prevent the seamline ending up at the peak of a pleat. When working the smocking, stitch through just the outer fabric and not the seam allowances.

A smocked piece could also be used as the outer section of a two-piece blouse cuff. Determine the amount of fabric that will be needed to pleat up the necessary length for the cuff. After the smocking is finished, flatten the pleats in the seam allowances by sewing across them with a zigzag stitch. Substitute button loops or snaps for machine buttonholes.

Pants, too, can be embellished with smocking. Choose a wide-legged design, a pull-on style in which the elastic casing at the waist is an extension of the pants front and back pieces rather than a separate facing. Use very lightweight fabric with good drapability.

At the waistline, use a stitch pattern that is elastic enough to fit over the hips. Incorporate "buttonholes" (described on page 58) so a ribbon belt can be woven through to snug up the waist.

Use an elastic stitch pattern at the ankle, too, so the fit will be loose enough to slip over the heel and instep. As an alternative, add plackets the length of the smocked design in the outside seams.

▶ Smocking shapes the area between waist and hips, eliminating the bulk that could result from simply gathering the skirt onto the bodice. The zigzag stitch pattern tapers off visually at its lower edge, a more flattering effect at the hipline than a straight horizontal line would create.

▲ On the back, fabric loops for lacing are sewn into the underlay seams.

◄ This subtle design, stitched in silk on sheer rayon chiffon, works well above the hipline. Smocking reduces the bulk of the fabric gathers with a stitch pattern that has adequate elasticity for the area where it is used.

Adding a Placket

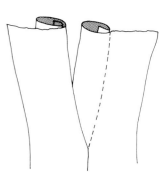

WHEN YOU CUT the skirt, add an extension to the left front and back pieces. Add approximately 2½ inches (6.5 cm) in width. In length, make the placket the length of the smocked design. After pleating the fabric, remove gathering threads from the extensions.

Turn under and press the outer edges of the extensions. Fold the extensions in half lengthwise so the pressed edge lies along the side seamline. Press again, and stitch close to the inner edges. When smocking has been completed and the side seam sewn, stitch the two extensions together across the lower edges and fold the front extension back along the seamline.

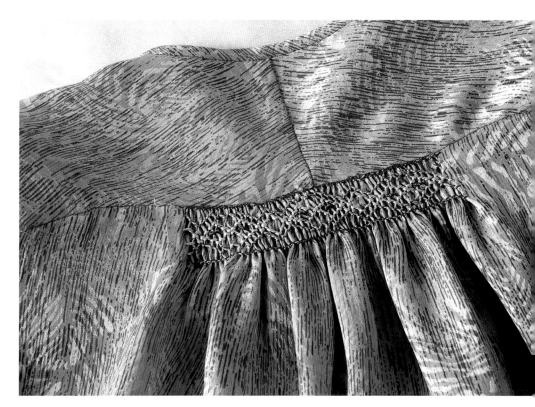

▶ ▼ This blouse pattern called for gathering at the front and back yoke seamlines and at the lower edge of the sleeve. Width of the front and back lower sections wasn't sufficient to work the smocking all the way across, so it was confined to center back and a narrow section on each side of the front. The substitution of a smocked design for routine gathering makes a much more interesting garment, and one that is uniquely yours.

SMOCKING PART OF THE WIDTH

A blouse, dressing gown, or nightgown pattern often will have a straight or curved seam above the bust in front and above the shoulder blades in back, with the lower part of the garment gathered or pleated onto the yoke. These areas are perfect places to substitute smocking for the gathers.

Usually, however, the lower section of the bodice will not have enough excess width that it can be pleated up and smocked all the way across. Pleat the entire width, then pull out the gathering threads to leave a pleated section just at the center of each front piece, or at each shoulder in the back. Remove an equal number of pleats from each side of the piece for symmetry.

A very full blouse sleeve can be treated in the same way. A narrow strip of smocking can replace gathers at the shoulder or at the cuff. The lower edge of the sleeve in this case probably will be curved, requiring some manipulation through the pleater to keep the pleats perpendicular to the edge.

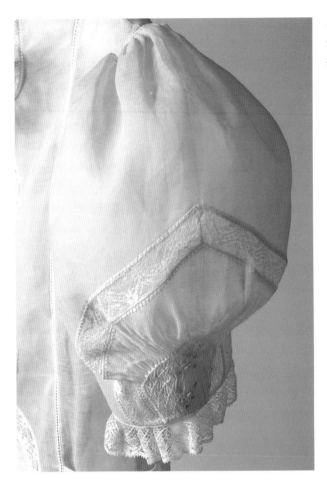

◀ The sleeve of this girl's dress was full enough that no additional width had to be added to accommodate the smocked design.

Altering the Pattern

WHENEVER YOU CUT and reassemble a pattern piece, work with a traced copy to preserve the original. Draw in all the seamlines and refer to those rather than the cutting lines when you are deciding where to place the new seams.

Mark the lengthwise grainline on the copy, and draw a line exactly perpendicular to it across the piece to indicate the crossgrain. Use the grainlines as the guide for placement of the new seams.

Draw in the new seamlines. Mark across each one at one or two points so you will be able to realign the pieces. Cut along the lines, then trace the pieces and add seam allowances. Extend the matching points to the cutting lines.

Always test the changes by quickly sewing up the altered pattern in inexpensive muslin. It isn't necessary to pleat the new inset, but do check that you are pleased with the placement of the lines.

It is usually a good idea to line an inset section. Besides providing a neat finish inside and hiding the knots, the lining serves to control and stabilize the smocked section.

Expand the piece to be used for smocking to the width that will pleat up to the finished size of the piece. For a piece that has curved lines, like the front inset below, it is easiest to pleat a rectangular piece of fabric cut to the needed width and to longest measurement of the inset. Mark the curved seamlines—the neck and lengthwise seams—onto the pleated fabric and work the smocking to fit within them. Then machine baste along the seamlines and cut the piece to fit.

ADDING AN INSET

Sometimes it isn't practical, or wouldn't be attractive, to widen the total length of a garment piece in order to include a smocked design. The pattern piece can be cut apart and reassembled with one of the sections pleated up and smocked. Smocked areas across the front of children's clothes often are handled in this way. It is interesting and not at all difficult to add an inset down the front of a dress or blouse with a back opening, or to create a separate yoke.

Piping is often added at seamlines around the smocked section. It defines the smocked area neatly, and the smooth seamline of the piping helps prevent the pleats of the smocking seam allowance from making an impression on the right side of the garment.

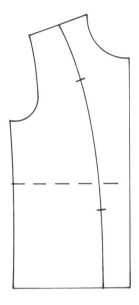

FRONT INSET

This front inset can be added to a dress or blouse pattern that opens down the back. Notice the new seamline curves very slightly at the bust. The center front line serves as the lengthwise grainline, and the crossgrain is shown by the dotted line.

► The inset front panel of this dress is smocked in a lattice pattern (page 50), which doesn't require the fabric width of smocking designs worked on pre-pleated fabric. For the sleeves, the pattern piece was widened as described on page 97.

◄ ▼ A separate front panel on the bodice of a wedding gown allows for the addition of a smocked design without sacrificing the graceful lines of the dress or adding bulkiness. The panel was pleated horizontally because the length of the piece exceeded the pleater capability. Since the dupion silk fabric of the gown is woven with heavier threads in the weft, or crossgrain, of the fabric, this trick worked beautifully.

SMOCKED YOKE

An existing yoke pattern piece can be used as a guide for the smocked area, or a yoke can be created from a one-piece front or back as shown. The simplest yoke is one in which the lower edge is perpendicular to the lengthwise fabric grainline. Plan so the seamline is approximately 2 inches (5 cm) above the fullest part of the bust. If desired, widen the lower part of the bodice by approximately 1 inch (2.5 cm) so that it can be gathered slightly at the yoke seam.

Cut a rectangular piece to pleat for the yoke, as described on page 90. Mark the neckline and armhole seamlines before smocking the pattern.

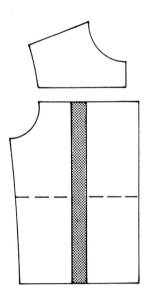

ADDING A ROUND YOKE

A round, or bishop, yoke accommodates a smocking design that radiates from the neckline of a dress, a nightgown or robe, a blouse, or for a jacket like the one on page 94. The smocked area might be restricted to just the front of the garment, or may include the back too. Follow the guidelines on page 90 to alter the pattern. Measure out from the neck seamline at closely spaced intervals so the yoke will be even in width all the way around. Remember to add seam allowances at the new seamline for all pieces.

Cut the lower front and back pieces as you normally would. Cut the yoke as a single piece, if possible, on the crossgrain of the fabric, with seam allowance top and bottom. The piece should pleat up quite tightly at the neckline edge to fit the seamline, and more loosely at the outer edge to fit the garment.

If the yoke can't be cut from a single fabric width, plan the seams to be at the shoulders. Stitch the shoulder seams before pleating the fabric. Trim the seam allowances. When you pleat the fabric, make adjustments if necessary so that a seam doesn't land at the peak of a pleat, but is within the pleat where it won't be visible. Sew the garment shoulder seams, then stitch the yoke to the garment before smocking.

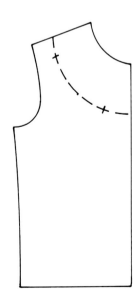

▲ For an elegant evening jacket in cotton velvet, lighter weight fabric of the same color was used for the smocked yoke. The smocking pattern is shown in detail on page 21.

SKIRT YOKES

A separate crossgrain section, pleated and smocked, can replace the upper several inches of a pleated skirt with great success. The smocked yoke will fit more snugly to eliminate the bulky look often resulting from unstitched pleats at the waistline.

Make shallow pleats, and use a fabric that will not pleat stiffly, or do both, to keep the fabric width to a minimum. Add a placket at the side as described on page 88. For the smocking, plan a pattern that doesn't create strong horizontal lines and that has a reasonable amount of elasticity.

▲ ▶ Rayon chiffon is light enough to work well in a smocked skirt yoke. The overblouse can be worn over a silk tee and left open to show off the pretty smocking pattern.

◄ A separate yoke, smocked tightly, makes for a smoother fit at the hipline than would pleating the skirt directly onto the waistband.

IRREGULARLY SHAPED INSETS

The photographs on page 25 show a smocked inset added to a jacket sleeve just for the design impact. Fabric for pleating was cut on the fabric crossgrain, like the round yoke above. Owing to the elastic nature of the pleated and smocked piece, it was an easy matter to curve it into shape.

The smocked piece was laid on the sleeve pattern and its seamlines marked. Seam allowance was added inside those lines to cut the adjoining pieces of the sleeve.

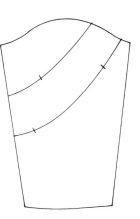

Widening a Pattern Piece

SOMETIMES IT IS EFFECTIVE to add width to the entire pattern piece to accommodate a smocked design. The guidelines for altering a pattern to add an inset (page 90) apply here, too.

BODICES

The front or back of a bodice can be cut to create a yoke, as shown in the drawing on page 93. The resulting lower bodice piece is widened so that smocking can be worked all the way across or just in a narrow area.

On a nightgown or robe, fullness can be added all the way across the front or back without ill effect. On a blouse, however, the fabric volume would be too great to tuck comfortably into a waistband. For a blouse, the better alternative is to plan just a narrow smocked section on each half of the front and back, or across center back, as illustrated on page 89.

SLEEVES

A sleeve can be widened enough for the addition of a smocked panel by cutting parallel to the lengthwise grainline from the uppermost point of the cap. The smocked panels shown on pages 43 and 91 were created in this way, as well as the picture smocking designs shown on 45 and 46.

On a long sleeve, smocking could extend the full length of the addition. For a very different effect, smocking might be worked just to slightly above the wrist, with the cap gathered to fit the shoulder seamline. (A)

It is possible, too, to add fullness for a smocked design to just the cap of the sleeve without widening the entire sleeve. The drawing illustrates how the sleeve cap of a dropped-shouldered garment can be slashed along the lengthwise grain. Open a wedge of the desired size and flatten the pleats that occur at the sides. Copy the pattern, using the original pattern piece to re-establish the correct length at the sides. Match the original lines at the underarm, blending them into the new ones. (B)

A wedge-shaped area can be added to the lower edge of the sleeve in the same way. Follow the lengthwise grain, and add the fullness at the back of the sleeve where the pleats or gathers are normally placed. (C)

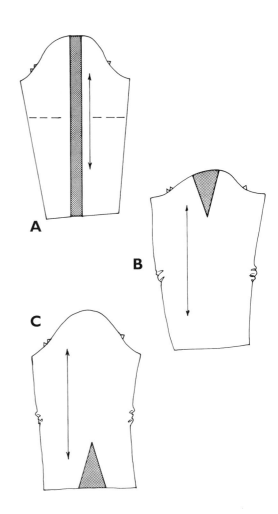

APPLIQUÉ

A smocked piece, worked to a size and shape that pleases you, can be applied on top of the garment section. Take care with the design so the piece isn't so bulky that it creates an unwanted third dimension. Baste the piece in place, then cover the raw edges with a folded bias strip or with any braid or trim that looks right.

In the blouse at right, lattice smocking, in the form of a small appliquéd V, adds an attractive design element at the neckline. The lattice pattern is worked on soft polyester fabric for a finished piece that isn't the least bit bulky.

Experimenting with Shapes

THERE ARE DOZENS of other places and ways smocking can be added to a garment with spectacular results. The pleater can be used to shape pieces of all descriptions. Smocking can take many forms and create a great variety of design effects.

Take some time to play with the pleater and different fabrics to see what ideas develop. Take inspiration from the photos here, but also from shapes and patterns that you see every day in magazines and books, as architectural elements, in nature itself. Don't throw away the unsuccessful attempts—one of them may be a starting point for your best design yet.

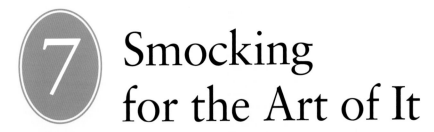

7 Smocking for the Art of It

Creating an art piece, just for the fun of it, offers a perfect excuse to try out decorative threads and interesting fabrics. There is no worry about fitting. Workmanship isn't important. Whatever the results of your experimentation, you will probably have acquired several ideas that can be incorporated into future projects.

Convex Dimensions

NELLIE DURAND

YEARS AGO, the creator of this piece developed the concept of applying smocking to round and oval shapes. Here she expands upon the theme, flattening and attenuating the ovals.

The shapes are smocked with cotton twist on natural linen, a subtle combination that emphasizes the stitch patterns and the shapes themselves. The ends are finished with variations of spiderweb stitch.

The Tijuana Bass

SARAH DOUGLAS

THE WATERY SHEEN of dupion silk makes an ideal background for a colorful sea creature. The two background colors, seamed together, were pleated with metallic thread and the gathering threads left in place to catch the light.

The fish itself is worked on pleated black wool flannel and stitched with a variety of threads. The fish was sewn onto the background after the embroidery was completed, the fins and tail left free to ripple with the currents.

Silk, wool, cotton, and metallic threads each contribute in a different way to the overall design. Smocking stitches, embroidery, and needle weaving are used in all kinds of combinations to give the piece its rich texture. Shisha mirrors, embroidered in place, add brightness and sparkle.

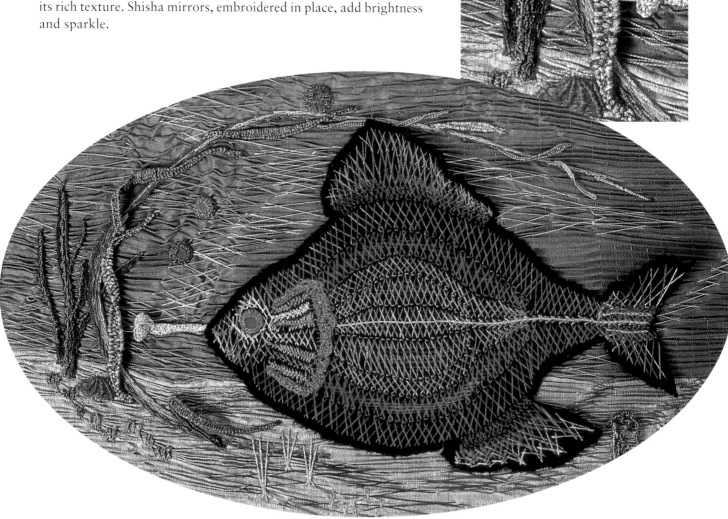

Vibrations

NELLIE DURAND

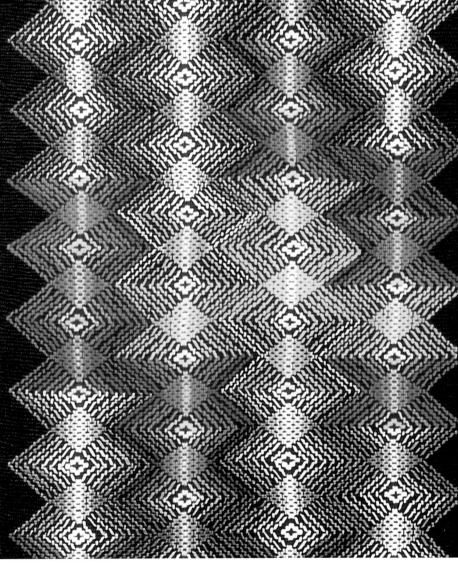

A WELL-PLANNED placement of colors produces the effect that gave this piece its name. The artist used a temperature contrast for the lightest and darkest values.

Just cable and small wave stitches were used, the pattern is perfectly geometric, yet the overall feeling is one of great strength and drama. It is worked on black linen with cotton floss. The idea for the piece was inspired by a stitch pattern the artist had seen years before on a baby dress.

Christmas Angel

REBECCA TODD

SILK FABRICS, lustrous dupion for the dress and sheer organza for the wings, were used to full advantage in the creation of this exquisite angel. Skirt and sleeve lining pieces were cut shorter than the outer fabric sections, then the two were stitched loosely together at the outer edges to produce rich puffs and folds.

The wings were fed through the pleater to develop their texture. Around the edges, silk ribbon is rolled around fine wire then whipstitched into place. Because the wings are transparent, their smocking pattern had to be identical on both sides. This required offsetting the design by half a stitch to compensate for the opposite peaks of the pleats.

Silk ribbon roses make up the angel's nosegay and garland; additional blossoms embellish the dress.

Reflects

NELLIE DURAND

PERIODIC COLOR CHANGES in precise rows of cable stitching create transparent, overlapping geometric shapes. Black cotton twist continues the cable rows between the colored forms to maintain a consistent texture. A dull metallic strand, laid along the top of each pleat within the colored areas, causes the colors to emit flashes of light when viewed from certain angles.

For the background, a non-reflective black wool fabric remains invisible behind the stitching. The colors and stitches seem to float above, detached from their surface.

Il Distrato

SARAH DOUGLAS

AN INCREDIBLE VARIETY of stitches and threads manipulate the small pleats of the silk noil ground fabric to produce a surface rich in textures and full of movement. Behind the face, vertical threads were removed along the valleys between the pleats of the background fabric and the opened areas hemstitched to create the feeling of great depth.

The piece is a portrait of a grief-stricken friend, yet it seems at the same time to convey a feeling of hope through its bold colors and strong lines.

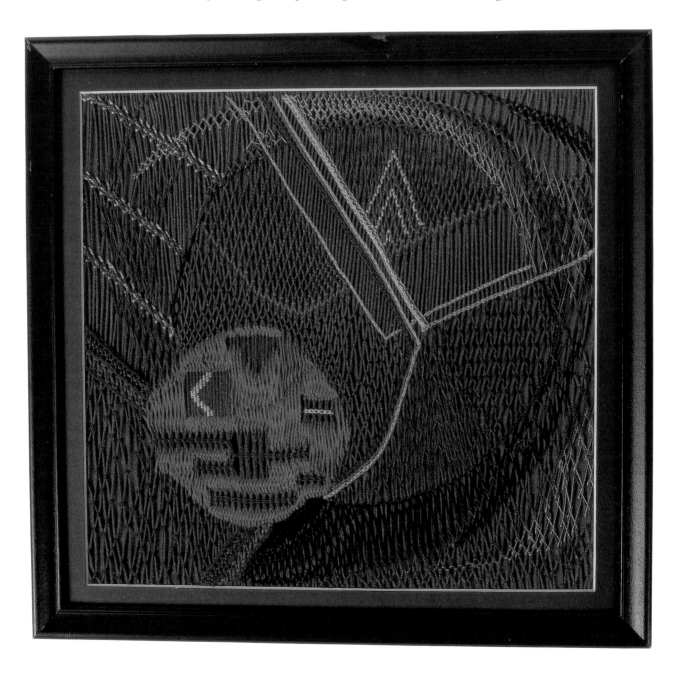

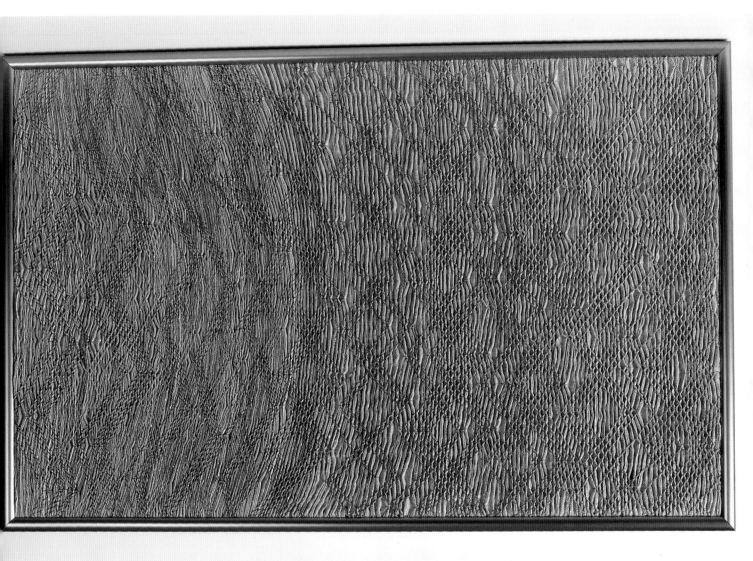

Breezes

NELLIE DURAND

A WALK PAST this enigmatic piece invokes a feeling of the breezes for which it is named. The muted colors and irregular stitch patterns seem to change direction, and fine metallic threads shimmer in the changing light.

Trellis stitch is worked vertically on a neutral chambray fabric, with strands of silk beaded under the smocking stitches along the peaks of the pleats. At left, the pleats are deliberately distorted, adding to the sense of movement.

The Frivolous Fowl

SARAH DOUGLAS

"IF A LITTLE ROUND THING IS GOOD, A BIGGER ONE MIGHT BE BETTER." With this thought in mind, the artist conjured up and brought to life a two-foot bird, species unknown, feathered in silk taffeta.

All kinds of pleater tricks were employed to shape the fabric around curves and to create textural interest. The silk is crisp enough to hold the pleats permanently after they were set with steam.

Over much of the surface backsmocking alone contributes the texture. Smocking on the surface with assorted colors and stitches defines the features and adds the bird's unique characteristics. The feet? Metal banding, wrapped with ribbon.

Another smocked creature might originate with a stuffed animal pattern as a basis. Made up in muslin and shaped to perfection, pleated fabrics can then be applied to fine-tune the shape and stitching added to supply the details.

Kaleidoscope

NELLIE DURAND

THE ARTIST HAS translated her fascination with kaleidoscopes into a stitched representation worked in three dimensions. It is smocked with traditional stitches in the manner of a bishop neckline, a woven spider web at the center. The vibrant colors dance and change in a most kaleidoscopic fashion.

The Old Woman Who Lived Under the Hill

SARAH DOUGLAS

A verse from childhood is brought to life in the most delightful way imaginable. Silk noil in two colors was pieced to create the background. Trapunto—stuffing from behind—gave shape to the hill and the woman. Shimmery rayon and silk threads for the stitching and shisha mirrors at the flowers' centers contribute to the lighthearted spirit of the piece.

Needleweaving, feather stitch, needle lace, French knots, and chain stitch all contribute their textural qualities. From the chimney float smoke rings in the form of silky thread loops.

ACKNOWLEDGEMENTS

We would like to thank the skilled smockers whose work appears on the preceding pages. They have provided not only inticing examples of their work for our enlightenment and inspiration, but have contributed tips and techniques gleaned from their years of experience.

MIMI AHERN, *of San Jose, California, developed a love of both teaching and stitching when she began a career as a home economics teacher. Since then, she has taught smocking workshops across the country. As a vehicle for play, she is partial to the round ornament for its minimal requirement of materials and its interest as a finished piece. Recently, one of her particular pleasures is experimentation with resist dyes and crayons on pleated fabric.*

Pages 29, 42 (right), 44 (upper), 56, 78–81

SARAH DOUGLAS *is a master at pleater artistry. For her, the pleater is perhaps even more valuable as a design tool than as a labor-saving device. She has taught workshops internationally on smocking and use of the pleater. Her articles have appeared in a number of publications and her book,* The Pleater Manual, *is available through smocking suppliers. Sarah enjoys enhancing the inherent texture of pleated fabric with a variety of hand needlework techniques and texture-rich combinations of threads. A background*

in costume design has led her to explore adaptations of clothing patterns for smocking. She lives in Orinda, California.

Pages 24, 44 (lower), 60, 63, 64, 100, 104, 106, 107, 109

NELLIE DURAND, *of Knoxville, Tennessee, is one of the founding members of the Smocking Arts Guild of America. She has been been an advocate of the craft for many years. Her work has won prizes in juried and invitational exhibits and has appeared in needlework publications internationally. She has taught smocking through classes for organizations and needlework shops across the United States and Canada, and through articles and columns in a number of publications. She particularly enjoys the artistic application of traditional stitches and materials, experimenting with the interaction of colors and shapes.*

Pages 20 (upper), 25, 27, 44 (center), 46, 47 (left), 51, 98, 99, 101, 103, 105, 108

DEBBIE GLENN's *designs have appeared in smocking publications worldwide. In addition to teaching, she designs for her own*

pattern company, Love and Stitches, *in Aiken, South Carolina. Her forte is clothing designs for women and children that feature charming combinations of smocking with other needlework techniques.*

Pages 18 (upper), 19 (upper), 20 (lower), 23, 26, 32, 43, 45, 47 (right), 50, 53, 65, 90, 91

SHARON KAST *is co-owner of a smocking and heirloom sewing shop in Fletcher, North Carolina. While she is a devotee of smocking, she also enjoys—and teaches—silk ribbon and other forms of embroidery as well as heirloom and French hand sewing techniques.*

Pages 33 (lower), 54, 66, 67, and the stitch examples shown in Chapter 3.

ALLISON SEILS, *of Parker, Colorado, developed the Contessa pattern line, featuring elegant smocked garments and accessories for women. Her designs have been featured in many publications. She is adept, too, at shadow work embroidery and has published her favorites in a collection entitled* Silken Inspirations: Shadow Work Embroidery Designs.

Pages 17, 18 (lower), 19 (lower), 21, 22, 30 (lower), 33 (upper), 37 (lower), 52, 55, 57, 61, 71–77, 83–89, 92, 94–96

REBECCA TODD, *Sterling, Virginia, is descended from a long line of needle artists. One of her ancestors organized a needlework school for women in North Carolina at the turn of the century, and Rebecca is currently re-creating a piece of the woman's silk ribbon embroidery from an old photograph. She teaches English smocking and other traditional handwork in the Washington, D.C. area.*

Pages 31 (lower), 38, 48, 49, 58, 59, 102

LORELEI TROUP *has a smocking supply business in Silver Spring, Maryland, where she designs smocked garments and accessories. She teaches smocking as well as other classic needlework techniques at her own shop and throughout the Washington, D.C. area. One of her successful students, daughter Katrina, stitched the balloon shown on page 39.*

Pages 68, 69

A NOTE ABOUT SUPPLIERS

Usually, the supplies you need for making the projects in Lark books can be found at your local craft supply store, discount mart, home improvement center, or retail shop relevant to the topic of the book. Occasionally, however, you may need to buy materials or tools from specialty suppliers. In order to provide you with the most up-to-date information, we have created a suppliers listing on our Web site, which we update on a regular basis. Visit us at www.larkbooks.com, click on "Craft Supply Sources", and then click on the relevant topic. You will find numerous companies listed with their web address and/or mailing address and phone number.

INDEX